# Building Bridges

## The Allyn & Bacon
## Student Guide to Service-Learning

**Doris M. Hamner**

*Institute for Community Inclusion*
*Boston Children's Hospital*

**Allyn and Bacon**

Boston ■ London ■ Toronto ■ Sydney ■ Tokyo ■ Singapore

*To Jose*

ISBN 0-205-31974-2

Printed in the United States of America
10   9   8   7   6   5   4                    03

# CONTENTS

# PREFACE

This book was written to provide the people involved with service-learning the preparation they seek, and the motivation to sustain them throughout their service-learning journeys.

The "mutuality" involved in doing service-learning influenced me while writing this manual, as I thought about the difference an energetic and concerned group of people could make I became more enthusiastic about making a difference myself.

The difference that I hoped to make is creating the first comprehensive and strategic guidebook for students who are engaged in service-learning. While students can gain much insight into the project by reading this book, it is not exclusively for students and it will also appeal to faculty advisors, campus placement coordinators, site supervisors, site clients, and school administrators who are considering offering service-learning opportunities at their post-secondary institutions.

The book offers a definition of service-learning, in order to more clearly understand the meaning behind these projects. It also details not only the benefits the student can gain from the service-learning but also the costs or the disadvantages of the project. These costs are helpful for the reader to offer preparation in advance if the student should discover any difficulties while working on the project, as the costs are combined with strategies to avoid undue conflict and problems.

The manual investigates the nature of the social service agency or community-based organization involved in the service-learning project to discover how the organization benefits from these types of projects. Another feature of the book is to specifically investigate the service-learners themselves by analyzing the typical characteristics of students who engage in community service.

Specific help is provided in order for the service-learning to find the right placement for them. The chapter on finding a placement offers the service-learner valuable assistance by giving the student an inventory worksheet to complete, and listing lots of different types of opportunities for them to consider.

The manual also offers a step-by-step guide on how to engage in service-learning while doing field research. Written by a qualitative researcher, this section gives the service-learner specific techniques to use to fit into the setting, and to write about the project. The book offers the reader insight into the meaning of reflection, and a guide to connecting the writing on the service-learning to the course. Also included are some common mistakes that are made by undergraduates when writing service-learning papers, with specific examples and strategies to use to avoid those mistakes.

The book concludes with strategies to use in order to work effectively within groups and offers advice on dealing with diversity. This diversity training is extremely helpful for individuals who find themselves ill at ease in different situations and who need to know how to best fit into any type of situation.

I have many to acknowledge. I would like to first thank Jose, my husband, who has encouraged me to get a Ph.D., write, and reach my potential since I first met him twelve years ago. Despite setbacks and family tragedies, he has never wavered in his support for my success.

James Ostrow, Ph.D., was my chairperson at Bentley College Department of Behavioral Sciences, was the first person to introduce me to service-learning, and showed me how to use it as a pedagogical technique in my courses. I am also eternally grateful to all the students at Bentley College who gave their time and effort to service-learning while taking my courses, and also showed me how important it was in their academic and personal journeys.

Also, Paula Sotnik of the Institute for Community Inclusion was a reviewer for the chapter on diversity and offered her many years of expertise in the field to this book. I am also indebted to Kathleen Jordan, Ph.D., and Shereen Tyrrell for giving me their unflagging encouragement. Also, thanks to Reverend Peggy Howell and the people of St. Anne's Episcopal Church in North Billerica, MA, for showing me how people can add to their community with an united team effort and lots of love. A special thanks to my grandmother, Theresa Costanzo, for always showing me how important it was to work for the greater good by repeating "one hand washes another."

# INTRODUCTION

This book is a guide for undergraduates to use when considering involvement in a service-learning project, and to use as a manual while they are participating in service-learning. It was written to give the prospective service-learner more insight into what these projects are like, ideas on what can be expected in terms of what s/he will encounter, and what type of writing will be expected of him or her. The goal is that by using this guide, the service-learner does not feel as though s/he is beginning from "ground zero," when s/he begins his or her service-learning participation, and that s/he has done enough preparation before the project begins and during it, so that s/he does not feel overwhelmed by his or her service-learning assignments. The service-learner can enjoy his or her experiences much more in these projects, if s/he has had some preparation beforehand.

The first important concepts to master are what service-learning is and how the undergraduate can benefit from the service-learning project. Here is a good definition of service-learning:

> We consider service-learning to be a course-based, credit-bearing educational experience in which students (a) participate in an organized service activity that meets identified community needs and (b) reflect on the service activity in such a way as to gain further understanding of the course content, a broader appreciation of the discipline, and an enhanced sense of civic responsibility (Bringle and Hatcher, 1995).

Through service-learning projects students learn through their participation in service, and they are also asked to meet the needs of the community. Service-learning projects are incorporated into the academic curriculum and provide students with opportunities for critical reflection. The student who participates in this type of a project is usually asked to connect his or her project with influential societal and civic issues and encouraged to be an active citizen.

In order to get a better sense of what service-learning is all about, it may be helpful to differentiate service-learning from volunteerism. In service-learning projects, as the definition implies, both service and learning are directly integrated into to the program. The service-learner, the community, and the academy are all intricately involved in a reciprocal relationship. The different parties are all expected to gain insights from each other and to benefit from service-learning. In the "typical" volunteer situation it is specifically the volunteer who is assisting the member of a social service organization. In service-learning situations it is all parties that are learning from, gaining insights about, and benefiting from the reciprocity in the relationships. The hyphen in service-learning is important in the definition because the hyphen represents the dynamic relationship between service and learning (Jacoby, 1996). It is the community who is defining its needs and is thereby empowered to establish the standards for the project. The reciprocity involved in the service-learning relationship relies on mutual responsibility and respect. The volunteer typically refers to someone who has more resources helping the unfortunate; the service-learner understands that s/he can gain a great deal from the social service agency as well as the member. There is a dynamic exchange between all parties as they work collaboratively with one another, which is the basis of the service-learning relationship. The volunteer experience can be described as a one-way street; the service-learning experience can be conceptualized as a two-way street. Both the learner and those who are served can be empowered by the experiences.

As Mintz and Hesser (1996) point out, there is an exchange occurring between the individual, the organization, and the academy, in which all three parties are teaching and learning from one another. Not only does the student share with those served, but those served also open up their lives to the student. For example, a homeless person may tell the college student about his or her life, and is thereby sharing important experiences and teaching the service-learner. In reflective writings on the experience the student can discuss the issue of personal "gain" and what the student, those served, and faculty member all receive from the project. You can also learn to take the perspective of those served, to learn more about their experiences, as they learn about yours. This expectation that both parties can benefit from the service-learning experience has also been referred to as "mutuality" (Rhoads, 1997). In fact, the reciprocity of the service-learning experience also extends to the faculty member who is enriched by having the project as a part of his or her course, as s/he learns about the community, and about social worlds outside the college.

The structure of this guidebook is organized around the different parts of the service-learning project as a process. It is organized so that the undergraduate can gain insight into what can be expected from the service-learner from the beginning of the project, until the conclusion of his or her paper is written.

The first chapter lists the benefits of the service-learning project for the students. It discusses how the students can improve themselves by engaging in service-learning and also how they can help others at the same time. This chapter describes what can be gained educationally and experientially by the service-learner specifically.

Chapter II focuses on the benefits of the service-learning for the community. Due to the "mutuality" involved, it is difficult to differentiate between the benefits to the individual and the community, but in this section the general emphasis is on how the community-based organization benefits from the service-learning project. This chapter refers to the community-based organization specifically, including the site supervisors and its clients. The section also delineates the benefits to the college, the faculty advisors, and the placements coordinators.

Chapter II also outlines the concerns and complexities involved when dealing with a community-based organization. The strain on the organization is emphasized here regarding some of the obstacles faced by these social service agencies. This section also features more about how to deal with awkward situations that might arise at the site.

The next section of the manual is devoted to understanding more about the costs incurred by the service-learners. It is helpful to determine in advance what the disadvantages are of the service-learning projects so that the students can anticipate them and prepare themselves. Certain strategies can prove to be helpful tools to avoid letting difficulties lead to discouragement and possible abandonment of the project.

The topics included in Chapter IV are on how to find a placement, tutoring as a service-learning experience, and some safety issues to consider while being involved in any service-learning project. The main focus here is on offering the potential service-learner many different ideas on what to do for a project. More specifically, tutoring is described as one possible alternative, and some research done on the impact of tutoring on undergraduates is summarized in this section. This chapter also includes a student inventory worksheet that the service-learner can answer to help determine what type of project would best suit his or her needs. Despite what type of service-learning project the undergraduate ultimately undertakes, this chapter concludes with a brief description of some important safety issues to be considered.

Chapter V provides some helpful techniques to assist the service-learner toward the successful completion of the project. This part of the manual acts as a trouble-shooting guide to use in order to get the most out of the project, while analyzing the site and obtaining all the objective facts necessary about the site, its clients, and its supervisors.

The next chapter deals with how to do field research, including specifics on writing a paper for the project. This part of the manual uses examples from students' papers to display how to best write about your experiences, and how to analyze your field notes. It also includes subsections on gaining acceptance at the site and how to interview at the site.

Chapter VII specifically deals with reflection to give the college student some suggestions on how to write a reflective paper. This is an extremely rewarding writing activity because the service-learner is encouraged to include his or her own ideas and feeling within the paper. This chapter also includes suggestions on how to make connections between the student's reflections and the content of the course while using actual student papers as examples.

The next chapter examines some common mistakes that the student makes when writing service-learning papers and how to avoid making those types of errors when writing. Two mistakes discussed are referred to as the "white knight syndrome" and "lecture regurgitation."

The final chapter of the manual investigates the topic of working in groups and how to best keep a group of people supporting one another and highly motivated. This chapter also deals with the topic of diversity especially in terms of helping the student learn from people at the site and in his or her teams who have different backgrounds.

The Web site, **http://ablongman.com/servicelearning** that is connected to this book contains three tables that investigate thoroughly the demographic characteristics of the students who engage in community service. In tabled form the percentages of the undergraduates involved in community service are outlined according to data collected by the U.S. Department of Education. The tables are described in a narrative form in and a "picture is painted" of the typical student who involves himself or herself in community service to a significant extent. The website also contains a list of helpful resources to investigate the wide range of service-learning opportunities available.

# CHAPTER 1

# Benefits of Service-Learning for the Student

If you are considering doing service-learning, you may be wondering what it entails exactly, and you may have to evaluate the benefits and the costs of the project. It is difficult to assess from the outset what the positive and negative consequences are in their entirety, because what you receive from the project will be unique to your own experience. However, this manual can identify for you what others have found to be the reasons for devoting their precious time and effort into the service-learning project.

Service-learning projects benefit the student because they are fun and a worthwhile effort. There are so many rewards involved it is easy to benefit from these types of experiences. Even when discussing the drawbacks to the typical service-learning project, those disadvantages can easily work for you, as far as preparing you for difficult situations in future life and work circumstances. Most important to remember before you embark on your service-learning journey is that **you can make a difference.** You don't have to be a certain type of person to make a difference, because all types of people can get involved and affect someone else's life in some way. If you are motivated and optimistic—people can sense your energy and eagerness to help. If you are not, if you dread meeting people, and are terribly shy in public, you may be astonished at what you can accomplish despite your fears. It has been the case, in my experience, that students who are shy, cautious, and reserved can also have excellent service-learning experiences. The typically quiet person, who is involved in the project, can make a difference in a quiet way—being a "people person" is not a requirement. Quiet students who are shy can have excellent service-learning experiences by talking to site members one-on-one or, perhaps, playing a board game.

As the student questions public issues and gains insights, s/he is also **taking risks.** S/he is leaving his or her own "comfort zones" of the typical social world of family and friends, and s/he is entering new domains. This risk-taking is a great learning tool because s/he will take his or her knowledge from course work, and see how it applies to different situations. Students can discover how topics such as inequality, racism, and ageism might explain different types of social situations.

**The service-learning project can help the student achieve a greater understanding of the course content.** By being involved in a service-learning project the student can learn how to build a bridge between the theory learned in a course, and see how it applies in practice. The service-learning project allows the student to test the theories s/he is learning in class, and use them to describe different life experiences. It is possible to use theory to help to understand the project you are engaged in, and subsequently enhance your learning and understanding of institutions, human relationships, and interaction. If you are able to bridge the gap between theory and practice through your service-learning, you have improved your ability to learn the course material. The course material will be more interesting and meaningful because you have been able to apply the course concepts to actual life experiences. You also may learn more about a particular area than you were previously aware of, for instance, if you have tutored in a service-learning experience, you may discover many different types of career opportunities in the educational field.

Service-learning is based on an educational philosophy that is different from the philosophy of the traditional classroom. Instead of educators providing facts, information, and concepts which the student is expected to learn in the service-learning classroom, the students can be encouraged to describe and analyze their feelings in the papers they write. Undergraduates are also asked to apply course concepts to these reflections. The reflective process, which includes empathy and empowerment for others, can be part of the service-learning assignment. When involved in service-learning, the student is learning in an active and participatory way that does not rely on passive and routine memorization.

What else can be gained from service-learning? It can build your confidence level to successfully complete a service-learning project. You might be able to tell others that you were able to do something you did not think possible or something that made a difference to someone else. You might discover that you are calmer in different types of situations because you were able to meet people in alternative settings.

You also could discover that you have a talent you did not realize, for instance, to be able to organize a service-learning event, or cook a meal, or teach underprivileged children. It can bring to the forefront a skill you did not realize you possessed. Further, you can build on skills you know by teaching others. For instance, you might know how to play basketball, and you can coach or teach children how to play at the local Boys and Girls club. The student can also learn leadership skills, because you could be in charge of dealing with different situations that you will be responsible for organizing and expediting. The undergraduates involved will need to show initiative during the project, and that learned initiative will help them in future projects they might need to lead. Other students within your team may look to you for advice and consultation; by offering it to them, you can be gaining experience for future endeavors in which you will have to be in charge, and it will also give you an increased sense of personal responsibility.

Furthermore, in these different situations you can grow as a person, develop an identity as a foundation on which you can base the rest of your life, and extend yourself cognitively, personally, and spiritually. You can mature socially as you learn that others will be dependent on your actions. The service-learning experience is a holistic endeavor because it can add to different aspects of college students of any age.

By learning new skills, and gaining leadership experience, the student can prepare for a future career path. For various careers, it is important to be able to motivate others, and to prove past endeavors in a leadership role. Unfortunately, it is difficult for college graduates to always have the kind of on-the-job experience that employers seek, but service-learning allows them to earn those credentials. Potential employers frequently seek individuals who are well rounded and can prove interest in the community. Service-learning is an excellent opportunity to work within different social service agencies, and to display an interest and expertise in organizations outside of the college campus. Service-learning with different types of organizations teaches you how they operate, and you can then decide what type of place you would like to work in full-time. You can also learn about organizational behavior and management, and what different institutions need to operate more smoothly and with greater efficiency. The service-learning experience can also lead to understanding more about how organizations are structured, how responsibilities are delegated, and how goals are accomplished. As the volunteer works within a certain setting, s/he can appreciate the internal operations of the institution. This added knowledge can benefit the student in different ways. S/he can become more experienced in what is efficient and not efficient in various situations, what types of leaderships skills are helpful and not helpful, and what type of authority structure is the most efficacious.

Not only will potential employers look favorably upon commitment by the student's participation in service-learning projects, but it may also lead you to network with those who have leadership roles, and who would like to work with you in a full-time position. By acting responsibly, and learning new skills, you can meet new people who may remember you for your good work and consider you for other types of positions.

The student maybe asked to offer solutions or organizational advice on operations at the community-based organization. For example, the student might discuss the advantages of a computerized accounting system, or an inventory tracking system, with the supervisor of a community-based organization. It is also possible that the student may be asked at some point to implement such a system in the agency. Such recommendations or structural reforms that could be part of a service-learning project can be negotiated between the student and the organization, including what level of responsibility the agency would like the student to have, and whether or not the student would like to offer such services. There is no end to the possibilities available if the student wishes to assume these types of tasks, and if the agency is open to the changes that are offered. These types of experiences can be crucial for the preparation of a student on a particular career path.

It may not always be the case that the community-based organization needs assistance, instead you may discover how many contributions a particular agency makes to the community, and be in awe of the far-reaching goals it has and is capable of accomplishing. Discovering the impact an organization has on the community, and the results of its efforts, are also rewards you can gain in the service-learning process. The student may have been unaware of the energy and enthusiasm some community-based organization members have toward improving the plight of many citizens.

Certain difficulties may arise during the course of the project; whether they are problems with the agency, staff, or fellow team members. Another advantage of service-learning is learning how to deal with these issues. Service-learning gives the student experience in solving problems, which is also a **guaranteed advantage in the workplace.** Not only does it assist the student in presenting her or him with skills for the future career, but it also aids the organization by helping it to run more smoothly for the sake of its members and employees. The service-learner can problem-solve and become skillful in the different coping strategies that will be imperative for themselves, as well as the organization. Learning to problem-solve in a creative manner, and learning adaptability, will be helpful both in one's personal life as well as in her or his professional preparation.

Problem solving is also associated with another skill that can be gained through service-learning—that is, decision making. Whether you are involved in a project alone, or you are part of a team project which is taking on a service-learning task, it will be helpful to make quick decisions on some phase of the project, without having supervisors available who can offer directions. Having to make quick, on-the-spot decisions will be a great skill to learn and exercise because this will give you the experience of "thinking-on-your-feet." In many business situations it is essential to be able to decide on the course of a project, or its possible resolution, quickly and without hesitation. There are not always people available at work to give you guidance, and you may frequently have to work independently. By providing decision-making experiences, service-learning will prepare you to be able to deal with these types of circumstances, and it can be a great advantage to be able to discuss these service-learning experiences on a job interview.

In addition to decision making, it is also helpful to learn communication skills during the service-learning project. Not only will it be helpful to communicate with other team members, but also you will have to sharpen your ability to interact with clients of the social service agency, and to discuss different issues with the employees of the community-based organization. You will discover that it is crucial, even if working independently, to make certain that all parties know about the decisions you have made, and what your goals are for your service-learning project. By learning how to facilitate agreement through communicating with other members of your team, and the site members, you will add to your consensus building skill. It is helpful if different individuals understand each other's perspectives when involved in service-learning tasks; it is actually in the act of communicating that learning can occur. When talking to other team members, employees of the social service agency, professors, service-learning site members, and service-learning center workers, you learn more about the actions and goals that are essential for the successful completion of the project as well as learning how to listen carefully. You will also learn how to solve problems in a creative way and to work collaboratively with your team members.

Another advantage of involvement in service-learning projects is diversity training. While on the service-learning adventure, you are likely to meet people you may not have met before; they may be from different countries, have various economic backgrounds; they could be any age, have varying educational levels, and even might be from more rural or urban areas than anyone you have ever met before. The diversity might also be found in the reasons or goals they may have for being at the community-based organization.

This does not imply that the service-learning student is a stranger to diversity, but only that this is a unique opportunity for all to be productive members of a team, that the diversity of the group can also add to what you can learn about one another, and from the situation in which you find yourselves. Being a part of a diverse team can offer a new perspective, and can expand the outlooks of the team members. Different perspectives can offer a new insight to solve a problem, or unique ways to learn the answers to mystifying questions. You can have a strengthened understanding of human difference and commonality as well as an openness to other ideas, empathy toward others, and a sense of social responsibility.

The people you will meet on a service-learning project can expand your informal and formal network as well as your own support system. Also, you can know for your own purposes that you are being an agent of social change, you are trying to make a difference in the world that surrounds you, and you may commit to including volunteer work in your future as part of your civic responsibility. Trying to make a difference allows you to identify for yourself, others, and the needs of oppressed people. By identifying these needs you have made them public property, which encourages change and solutions rather than oversight and neglect. The service-learning projects can bring about an investigation of complex social problems, and give the college student a deeper appreciation for the enormous obstacles these community-based organizations encounter, in addition to the site's clients. As you form reflective analyses, you may also be led to solutions and a deeper understanding of various issues, as well as having an improved understanding of their place in the United States and the global community.

Discovering the needs of community members can begin a very significant period of critical examination for undergraduate students. During this period, you not only think of others, but you also can reflect on how the oppressed are influenced by different features of the world around them, whether it is unemployment, racism, or poverty. You can gain rare insight into the nature of current events and their direct or indirect impact on the underprivileged. Perhaps you might not have realized before the true influence of political leaders, immigration policies, or public corruption, for example, but these service-learning projects can indicate the wide-ranging impact of these factors.

Service-learning can lead to values development. Students can learn about the problems faced by the community-based organization's clients, and they can learn that there are volunteers who are working to eradicate those problems. In some cases, there are people who have dedicated their lives to solving problems through these social service agencies, and they do not even get paid for their labor. It is always inspiring to meet people who are willing to give up profitable careers to help others which may not prove to be as economically lucrative. These people can become role models to students, thereby giving students support and encouragement and might affect the student's morality. The service-learner might consider and reconsider what competencies they would want to develop as a part of their career path.

The service-learning project can teach both individual development and group responsibility. While accomplishing tasks that can help others, you have contributed toward your own maturity and intellectual acumen. In this process the service-learner can learn from the people s/he has served, and the client is also likely to have learned from the service-learner. Service-learning can increase the student's abilities and skills by dedicating himself or herself to others. The student's individual development is enriched by an education into social responsibility. The individual and the society need not be separated by walls. Through service-learning the individual and the society are not antithetical to one another, but they grow through mutual appreciation and application. In this way, a sense of autonomy is increased and, at the same time, the service-learner can get involved in interdependent activities that are guided by collective goals.

One of the counterintuitive consequences of service-learning is that you might have begun the task with others in mind, but you have also gained personal fulfillment and growth in the process. As previously stated, you might not have realized how well you could do in certain situations. Perhaps you have a talent for teaching children that previously went unrecognized. It is possible you are an excellent leader, or dynamic public speaker, but because those skills were untried, you are more aware of them after the service-learning project. Further, there can be personal growth in terms of realizing that you have tried to reach out to others and have made a difference. In the process of being involved in service-learning, you can be a person who achieves a greater understanding of the world. You may not have realized before the opportunities that exist. The experiences in service-learning can give you a great sense of personal satisfaction.

In addition to a sense of personal fulfillment, you can also grow intellectually and morally. You can learn more through reflection, critical examination, and self-scrutiny about a variety of topics. Those involved in service-learning discover that the service allows them to think less about themselves and to transcend their daily worries. By getting away from their typical "world" and entering another domain, the service-learner can discover a way to forget about their own daily worries by connecting with others. The service-learners are taking great strides toward transcending the problems of life by actualizing values, contributing to something larger than themselves, and going beyond their own personal identity.

In sum, there are many reasons to be engaged in service-learning projects. The benefits have been outlined in this section of the book, but they can be combined by describing service-learning as an experience which allows you to reach out to others, as you simultaneously learn more about yourself. Service-learning is one of the few educational experiences which can afford you the opportunity to make a difference regardless of what type of person you are—shy, boisterous, calm, or anxious. It can allow you to observe the impact of larger societal issues on the individual in a community, and at the same time you are learning by extending yourself, taking risks, and learning by **doing.** Service-learners can prepare for their careers by increasing their networks, learning organizational behavior, doing problem solving, making decisions, improving communication skills, receiving diversity training, and at the same time, reexamining their lives.

Before you start your service-learning project you need to ask yourself—is this an activity that is worthwhile for you?

# CHAPTER

## 2 Benefits of Service-Learning for the Community

Through involvement in service-learning projects, the students are not only helping themselves, but they are also helping others. The service-learning project can help both student and site client to question taken-for-granted assumptions they might have about others, and to realize they are not alone in the world, but that there are others who are willing to share insight and experiences. In the interactive process, knowledge is gained about dealing with all kinds of people. The student can gain insight into how public issues such as housing, drug addiction, mental illness, high cost of living, unemployment, public policies, and domestic violence affect another's private troubles.

Through service-learning experiences we are making connections with other human beings. We are not having our own isolated experience but we are sharing experiences with others. In fact, people are working together and realizing that they can achieve the twin goals of mutual respect and understanding. Through service-learning projects students and site clients discover that they have more in common with each other than they had originally anticipated. In fact, with the increasing tuition rates and the declining numbers of subsidies, the students may realize that they could also face possible financial crises that some site clients confront.

The client of a community-based organization can also gain much from the service-learning project. S/he can discover there is hope in the world, and it is possible to meet a person who cares about him or her. They can also come to realize that there are others who share opinions, hobbies, or interests that they do, and are willing to share some time and offer some assistance.

One of the advantages of having college students work for a social service organization is to offer it specific and targeted assistance at no economic cost. In fact, one on-line resource states that volunteers are worth $12.84 an hour (**http://www.fsu.edu/~voluntee/funfacts/funfacts.htm**). Also, there is research which indicates that the National Association of Counties found that volunteers have provided $1.8 billion worth of services to U.S. county governments in 1992 (Markwood, 1994).

While the members of a social service agency might be overworked and underpaid, or unpaid, they need volunteers as much as possible. This type of active assistance can make the difference between an organization achieving its objectives or not being able to survive at all. In fact, some social service agencies are run almost entirely by unpaid workers. There are cases where certain programs have had budgetary cutbacks and/or have been downsized in some way so that the only way the agency can exist is through service-learning projects and/or volunteerism.

Service-learning projects can alleviate some of the pressure from the primary employees of a social service agency by offering various types of assistance. In cases where staff cuts are *de rigueur,* this extra help can relieve the agency of some of its burden. Ultimately, the service-learning helps not only the agency, but also its clients directly. For instance, when teaching is a service project, such as in America Reads or Junior Achievement programs, classroom teachers are alleviated of the pressure of dealing with an entire class in which students have varying skill levels. Also, after training from service-learners, the students can fit into the class better because they will have improved skills. In regard to tutoring, the undergraduate can teach the high school or elementary students theory as well as mentoring them, being their role models, and offering them individual support and encouragement.

The undergraduates can offer the community-based organization assistance in terms of helping with different projects, and offering advice about new ventures. Students can also offer practical expertise learned from courses that could improve the agency's productivity level, and its employees' skills in various areas. The undergraduates who have committed to a longer period of time with the organization can help to complete longer-term projects. For example, if a college student is majoring in accounting s/he might offer to improve the organization's accounting system. Also, the organization can benefit by sharing the resources of the college and university, and having the community-based organization's members use the campus facilities.

There are also some added benefits to service-learning for the community organization that are more indirect, such as the student offering reports on the status of the agency from an outsider's point of view. Some students may allow the members of the organization to read their reports. The confidentiality and anonymity of the clients and students are reserved, but the reader can discover different facts about the clients and the functions of the organization that were not readily apparent. If the organization's leaders and decision makers agree with these reports, then it is possible that changes can be made when possible. At times, outsiders can observe certain trouble spots, or vulnerabilities of the clients, which the person who has worked in an agency is not exposed to on a daily basis. It is also possible that clients may feel more comfortable talking to and confiding in students rather than the leaders of a community-based organization.

These different views of the organization, and reports that the students may provide, offer the agency new perspectives. Service-learners offer the organization a broader perspective of the organization and new ideas and energy on how to deliver services or to begin new services. Students provide new points of view and their own diversity to the staff. An organization has a regular set of volunteers, but college students can offer clients and the organization with different types of solutions to problems, and new people to meet. On yet another level, the client of the service organization may change their previous misconceptions about young people after being exposed to them during the service-learning project. If they did have a stereotypical notion of college students, they can have a changed conception on young people after being exposed to them in new and exciting ways.

Social service agencies may be willing to accept service-learners to join their staff for the diversity and targeted assistance offered by the students. If service-learning programs can change the minds of individuals about the people they serve, this would benefit the community-based organization. Many individuals who work at social service agencies are frustrated with public opinions about the client populations they serve. Preconceived ideas can provide people with skewed ideas of others and what they represent. These ideas may then also lead to the lack of understanding by the public of certain issues, as well as an unwillingness to fund social service programs. Service-learning can combat that unending cycle of ignorance and hatred, and replace it with understanding and caring. In the long run, these community-based organizations can be greatly benefited by service-learning projects that affect the public opinion of various groups, whether it is a population of homeless people in need of shelter, or the elderly in nursing homes. In this way the community-based organization is being active in the teaching and learning processes.

The advantages of the collaboration between the social service organization and the colleges are numerous. The connections forged between the university and the community organizations allow for more collaboration and less conflict. The college can go beyond isolationism and be able to establish strong bonds with the community. The college is able to add on service-learning sites for the students as these connections are forged. Further, the faculty members are able to discover new opportunities for research and teaching that meet the needs of the surrounding community (Jacoby, 1996).

This section outlines the reciprocal nature of service-learning projects, that is, how students and faculty affect community and also how the community adds to and expands the knowledge base of the college. The interaction that is formed between the individuals, the service-learner and the client, is the foundation of this relationship. As bonds are forged between individuals, so too, can connections be built between community and college. We can all be reminded of the fact that the adversity that affects one of us, affects us all, and unless we realize the importance of helping each other, our futures are uncertain.

## The Nature of Social Service Agencies

As mentioned previously, the workers at a social service agency are usually very busy and quite overworked. At times, they are underpaid and it is also possible they are strictly unpaid volunteers. It is therefore difficult for them to offer extensive training programs to prepare college students to come in and offer services to their clients. The organization, which is already likely to be overwhelmed with referrals, is also spending time and resources to train students and organize their visits. The service-learning visits are creating a burden to the organization in that they may find it time-consuming to establish some type of training for the college student.

It is helpful to note that you are entering into a partnership that will require a balancing between your abilities and their needs. You may not walk in knowing everything about what you will have to accomplish at the site, so it will be necessary to learn as much as possible in a brief period of time. Both the community-based organization's members and the service-learner will come to recognize that the interaction between the student and the organization is a two-way process. It is therefore necessary to work toward acceptance and reciprocity in the relationship.

The social service agency may be more structured for the volunteer rather than the service-learner, which may place additional time pressures on the student. For example, the organization might have practice in training volunteers who will then donate a certain number of hours for months, or maybe years. Students are usually only available for shorter periods of time: Their projects are usually based on the semester, which lasts approximately 4 months. This means that the social service agency needs to have more frequent training sessions and there is more pressure for the student to know what s/he is doing quickly, so that s/he can contribute to the organization. In some cases the student may be at the site for only 20 hours a semester, and it may take 10 hours for the student to be trained in how to accomplish certain tasks, which leaves only 10 hours to actually complete the work project. The quality of the service-learning experience will improve if the student is able to spend more time at the site. This is primarily because it does take time to be trained, or to learn how the agency operates, and to pay attention to the details and atmosphere of the community-based organization.

If a social service agency does not discern any difference between service-learning and volunteering, then it would be helpful for the site members to learn more about the objectives of the student's project especially in terms of its connection to the academic program. The objectives of the placement can be described fully in a service-learning contract, which can be written by the student and the site supervisor. It would assist the student if the organization's members knew what type of support s/he would have to offer, and also for them to be aware of what the college means by *service-learning* and what expectations the professor has for the student. If the student is representing himself or herself, rather than being represented by a faculty advisor or campus placement coordinator, s/he may have to discuss the objectives of the project with the site supervisor. The service-learner can feel at ease discussing the project's objectives with the social service agency, because the student is primarily interested in donating his or her time and effort to the agency, and simultaneously hoping to learn from its members.

The introduction the student makes to the social service agency is a good time to clarify the parameters of the assignment so that the site supervisor is familiar with the deadlines the student has, in addition to what type of paper the service-learner will be responsible for writing. If the site manager knows more about the assignment, this knowledge assists both service-learner and site members, because the site members will know exactly what the goals are, and can help the student and site clients to combine forces to achieve those objectives.

Social service agencies can be at different phases as far as being prepared for the service-learning project. The spectrum of preparation can include a very structured training process that is very organized for the service-learner, and may also have an orientation program established. Another phase may be an agency that is more unstructured in which they are small and understaffed and are not quite sure which role the service-learner will play. The general rule is that if there is more structure present, and the organization's members are well prepared for service-learners and have past experience offering these programs, then the student will have a more organized experience. If the organization does not have this structure, the students need to be flexible and "think on their feet" more about what needs to be done in different situations. The personal style of the service-learner is also an important factor that will guarantee the success of the project. The student may be more comfortable in an arena with structure and organization, and yet another service-learner might prefer a more informal and less structured environment.

The success of the service-learning project will be affected by the fit between the student and the social service agency; therefore, any background information the student can discover about the agency will prove helpful. Discovering the structure type, formal or informal, can help you to decide in advance if you will feel comfortable there. If you prefer more of an informal and less organized program, a good recommendation is to find out ahead of time what that atmosphere is like within the agency. It would also be helpful to discover if the site managers have any specific expectations for their service-learners, and assess if the service-learners fit in with these criteria. It may also help to see if there are any writings or pamphlets that the organization distributes which may help the student to ascertain if s/he would be satisfied with your project in this type of organization. The student can also refer to the website directory for this book found at **www.ablongman.com/servicelearning** to find a brief overview of many community-based organizations.

Some of the most reliable resources for information on an organization are your own perceptions when you enter it, and perhaps speaking to a site supervisor who can give you more information as to the way the agency is managed, and what s/he requires of service-learners. The organization's members will be willing to tell you what type of training is offered, or if there is any training offered. The best way to combat fear or intimidation at the outset of the project, is to have *information*. If there is a service-learning center on campus, then the center's coordinators should be able to offer the student substantial advice, if you do not have a center, then asking the agency's workers, or your professor, will assist the student by having an increased knowledge base.

Even if the student is prepared with information about the site and the service recipients, s/he still may be feeling vulnerable, which is natural because s/he will want to offer as much as possible to the site clients. Also, the agency employees are offering the student time and training to learn more about what goes on at the site, and the student should try to be accommodating and flexible. However, at a certain point, the students may not feel as though they were doing the tasks they were supposed to do at the community-based organization. Between this vulnerability, wanting to fit into the social service agency, and at the same time, wanting to be flexible and accommodating the needs of the organization, how should the student deal with tasks that are not part of the original service-learning agreement? For instance, if the student is asked to mop floors or paint the walls, but s/he was originally supposed to help with dinner, how should s/he deal with this new situation?

One possible way to deal with this awkward situation is to say your assignment at the site calls for more personal interaction than is possible when involved in the other tasks. You could also say that you would like to help, but that it would not be possible for you to be able to adequately complete the assignment that your professor has outlined if you got involved in other activities. It might also be helpful to offer your assistance in terms of putting in a request for other students to get involved in those duties with the campus placement coordinator, or to offer to ask your friends if any would be willing to do the extra work for the community-based organization.

The relationship between service-learning and the community-based organization is one marked by reciprocity: Each party offers much to each other in terms of learning opportunities and increased understanding of the community. If both groups offer each support and understanding, flexibility and accommodation, there is a limitless amount of information they can learn from each other, and countless acts of kindness which are possible. If barriers are placed before the service-learner, there are also strategies to see them coming, or quickly defuse them when placed before you. It is easier to solve smaller problems before they become large obstacles.

# 3 Costs for the Service-Learner: Strategies for Avoiding Difficulties

This section offers a general synopsis of the difficulties associated with some service-learning projects, and also includes ways of coping with those difficulties according to the student's perspective. One of the negatives associated with service-learning is feeling a sense of uselessness at some point, when s/he does not feel as though s/he is making a difference. This can also be categorized as a helplessness, or a feeling that no amount of service will alleviate the problems some people face. These emotions can combine to feel like "burnout" and can also be associated with a weariness or lack of energy, a cynicism, or depression.

The student who feels burnout may consider enjoying another type of activity that is considered restorative, such as a sport or hobby. Trying to relax, and doing something restful, will offer some rehabilitation. It is also helpful to tell yourself that you have done all that you can, and that you have not turned your back on others. Try to, whenever possible, accentuate the positive, think of the differences you have made, and the people you influence.

It is also interesting to note that some of the frustrations with the project do not necessarily come from the actual site visits, but from the organizing done prior to the site visits. For instance, ascertaining correct dates and times, confirming with other students, or clarifying transportation schedules are all time-consuming activities that may not seem complicated but can become cumbersome. Burnout can come from unlikely sources, so if there is a little nuisance that comes up, it may help to take care of it before it becomes a larger problem.

It may be that the college's Service-Learning Center is the source of some difficulties. The center may have to change projects suddenly due to "unforeseen" circumstances, or the student may be dealing with disorganized center members who are not clear on certain important details. Students sometimes find that some faculty members can be frustrating when it comes to not offering them clear advice on how to conduct the project. Figuring out a writing assignment, and how it will be assessed for a course, is easier if the student can offer the faculty advisor a rough draft of the paper. Connecting the service-learning to the course is one aspect that can be improved with the advice of the professor. Taking the time to write a rough draft can help the student write a good paper, get a good grade for the work, and also enhance the learning process.

Before the writing commences, it is possible that the students may encounter some difficulties with the staff of the social service agency or the goals of the agency itself.

Some students have discovered that when involved in a service-learning project, they may not be helping the people they were hoping to help. The agency may make the claim that its primary goal is to alleviate the problems of its clients, but it may seem to perpetuate the very problems it is hoping to solve. If an agency feeds the homeless, and offers them shelter, but does not help them find a place to live or employment, then it does not seem to be improving the situation as much as it is supporting the status quo.

There are ways to target the people the student wants to help through service-learning at the right type of organization. The service-learning should occur in a social service agency dedicated to social action to change the causes of certain social ills. Some organizations that actively pursue solutions are feminist groups, unions, or environmental organizations. If the course includes discussion and reflection exercises that link up the service-learning to the course concepts, the service-learners can reflect on what it means to be "doing good" (Strand, 1999).

Another possible drawback to the service-learning project is that, if unprepared, the student may have some preconceived ideas reinforced about the persons s/he is visiting. Some students come to class with ideas that can be described as "blaming the victim." This refers to placing the responsibility of the person's situation on that person, rather than offering social explanations. For example, a student may write that s/he finds the homeless people s/he meets are best described as "lazy," rather than paying attention to such factors as unemployment rates or deindustrialization (Hironimus-Wendt and Lovell-Troy, 1999).

The best preparation for avoiding blaming the victim is to take account of the outside influences the individuals have encountered through their life course, including all of the cultural, historical, or political events that have transpired that negatively affected the person's life chances. In so doing, the person becomes less of a victim of their own mistakes, as previously thought, and more of a victim of difficult, if not impossible, life circumstances. With permission from service recipients, it may help to conduct some life history interviews, to investigate some of the conditions site clients have lived and survived through. In this type of assignment, students can appreciate the persons they meet as survivors rather than victims. The life history interview can give the student a broadened perspective for all of the experiences (i.e., hunger, poverty, death in the family, racism, etc.) the person has lived through, rather than focus on individual problems as explanations for their need for service.

It would be helpful to choose a situation in which the student finds it easy to relate to the client of a community-based organization. If you can put yourself in the other person's situation with ease, you will be able to take the role of the other and empathize with the service recipient.

By appreciating the perspectives and positions of others it will facilitate the student's ability to empathize. It can help to clarify what a person is going through by imagining yourself in his or her life, trying to determine what the person has been through, as well as the external limitations on their opportunities. Try to think about these different scenarios and imagine yourself acting out the various situations. This can help you to determine the similarities you have with others, and how the differences may be related to unanticipated consequences.

Some students may have a difficult time figuring out how they can help the community, how to make a difference. Other students may assume they are experts and feel that it is their job to be involved, and change the social landscape. In either case the student who is prepared to take the perspective of another person will be ready to act responsibly in ways that can work in reaching out to others.

For those students who do not know how they will be contributing to others, it is helpful to note that students who assist those in need can contribute to improving the life chances of others, and that the service-learning project will probably be considered rewarding and worthwhile to service-learners and site clients. Even if students feel they do not have the necessary skills, they need to know that extensive experience is not required in order to reach out to others. There are people involved in service-learning who have made a difference, but did not begin the project knowing everything they needed to know to alter social inequities.

One of the possible drawbacks to service-learning is if the clientele at the site becomes the group that has the lowest priority in the project rather than the highest (Eby, 1998). It can be possible that professors become interested in how the project fits into the course; students are intrigued with the advantages that the project affords them, whether it is for their résumé or for increased course credit. The college or university also profits from the advantages of gaining improved status in the community, and this benefit may be paramount to the members of the educational institution. In light of all the advantages afforded the students, professors, and educational administrators, the purposes and goals of the site can become lost, and the needs of the people to be served can be lost in the shuffle. This possible disadvantage can be turned around by constantly keeping the community-based organization the focus of the work. Communication with the site supervisor can be done by the faculty advisor, the service-learning coordinator at the college, or the student, and those involved can share information on how the project is going, and improve the service-learning activity as part of a "feedback loop" between the people involved in the project.

Feedback on how the service recipients are feeling during the project can help to avoid another disadvantage to service-learning, which is if the site members feel as though they are in a "fish bowl," or that they have become objectified and are part of a project without being able to make a decision in what happens. Avoiding this type of problem involves respecting the norms of the people you are serving. This includes giving the service recipient the right to his or her own privacy.

Ask the campus placement coordinator, faculty advisor, or supervisor at the site what norms you should be aware of when preparing for the service activity. You may be serving people who have different socioeconomic or ethnic backgrounds than yourself. It is helpful to be sensitive to the norms of the persons receiving service. Try to conform to the expectations of the community in order to get more from the project.

You may notice that service recipients are more comfortable speaking with students about their lives than they are with site supervisors. This can be because the students are providing a valuable service, and the service recipient feels comfortable with them. It is important to keep the identities of the clients confidential and be sure they realize that what they say to you will be kept confidential. Even though the student will be writing about the client in his or her field notes, their identities will be concealed. The student's report will be used for the sole purpose of the service-learning project.

It is advantageous to recognize that service-learning is a complex task and no one is assuming that the organization is deficient or that the client has deficiencies, which is a common assumption for some (Eby, 1998). The assumption that a person is deficient, individualizes the need, meaning it directs us to blame the individual for the problem, or blaming the victim, rather than focusing on broad social problems.

The assumption of the deficiency of the person being served by the community has another effect on the service-learning project. The effect is that the student may feel somehow superior to the site member and may feel a need to improve them. The service-learning is an equal exchange rather than a superior assisting an inferior, and it is possible that blaming the victim can interfere with this delicate balance.

There have been a few themes that have been repeated throughout this section on the costs to the service-learner. One is that it is important to keep a clear communication process going between the student and an objective party throughout the project. If the student encounters difficulties with the site supervisor or the project, the best strategy is to reflect on what is happening, and discuss it with someone outside the agency such as the faculty advisor.

A second theme is that when there are small problems that come up during the project, they should be dealt with immediately. If difficulties can be dealt with when they appear, or in the beginning phase of the project, they can be defused before they become much more cumbersome to solve. It is clearly never too early to problem solve.

Third, if the service-learner experiences any form of burnout, uselessness, frustration, or exasperation, it is helpful to reflect on the positive aspects of the project and to communicate those dissatisfactions with the faculty advisor. It can help to begin the project with clear expectations and realistic goals about what can and cannot be accomplished at the site. It is possible that the service-learner can begin by thinking s/he can make a big difference, but may be exasperated by the complexities of the problems s/he faces. The clearer expectations can prevent the student from being disillusioned early on in the process.

Most importantly, the service-learner needs to pay attention to the importance of the service recipient in the project. Ensure that the focus remains on the clients and keep them as the focal point of the service-learning, while also making sure there is an equal exchange of information shared by both service-learner and service recipient.

It is possible to deal with these difficulties before they become too complicated, and therefore get more fun out of service-learning. The next section is devoted to understanding more about yourself before deciding on a project.

# 4 Finding a Placement

If your college has a service-learning placement center, this would be a good place to begin your search to obtain information on opportunities in service-learning. Investigating the different sites available can give the service-learner a better sense of the range of agencies available. The service-learning coordinator at the placement center on campus can answer questions you may have on the details of the service-learning project, the site itself, and your role in the organization. Try to determine what information you can discover on the exact duties you will be asked to do, what types of skills will be required, how many hours will be necessary to complete the project per week, and also, what insurance is available for students. Determination of insurance coverage will help to discover if you will be held accountable if there are any accidents at the site.

There may be an orientation program at your college organized by the service-learning placement center which may include a description of what service-learning is and a list of the different projects available in your community. An ideal orientation program may involve a number of representatives being present from different community organizations so that the student can discuss the organization directly with the site's supervisors.

Any information which can be gathered about the site itself will prepare you for a site visit, and also help to confirm for you if this is the best site for your current skills, abilities, goals, and interests. Details on the site will be helpful when preparing for your first site visit, or if necessary, an intake interview. You can then ask questions on the operation of the social service agency, if it is publicly or privately funded, and you can ask about its primary mission.

If you will be working with a faculty advisor during your assignment, it would be a great idea to try to ask him or her how the service-learning project fits into the course. Try to examine the expectations of the faculty advisor including how often you will meet, what type or if writing is required, and what are the academic objectives of your project. See if the professor would prefer to be actively or indirectly involved in the project. For instance, you might ask the professor if s/he will be going on the site visits with you, if s/he discusses the projects in class, and how the project will be evaluated in regard to coursework. How involved you would like the faculty advisor to be can affect what you get out of the project. You may be left on your own by a "hands-off" advisor, which may be adequate, or you may need the support of a "hands-on" advisor. How central the professor makes service-learning to the course can affect your experience and is partially dependent on your experience level and personal style. If the professor does not, for instance, offer group discussions in class in regard to what you are getting out of the project, the student may not have access to the type of information and advice that can be retrieved from group discussions. The previous section on self-evaluation can help you to decide which style you would prefer.

It will also be helpful to know in advance if you are going to the site alone or with a group. Both types of projects allow for different benefits. If you are going alone your independent status will allow for more learning about the site in less time. You are likely to be placed in a situation in which it is necessary for you to "sink or swim" quickly. In other words, you will not have anyone else to rely on to discover details about the site. If you are involved in a group project you will be able to depend on others for assistance so this will allow for more group discussions and interdependence on others. Once again, your personal style and experience level affects what you do or do not find important.

If you decide to embark on the service-learning project without the assistance of a placement center, or if there is no center on your campus, you will have to ask social service agencies directly if they would need someone who can provide the types of services you offer. Other types of off-campus resources that you can contact for information are volunteer clearinghouses that can connect you to various organizations that are found in the yellow pages of the phone book. There are also clearinghouses that are listed in the website directory for this book that can be found at **www.ablongman.com/servicelearning.** There are also service-learning centers from other colleges that work to place students as part of a consortium.

When you visit the site, try to observe if this is a place in which you can feel comfortable and learn at the same time. Also, try to discuss with a site supervisor about the projects s/he has available. There are some questions which you can ask which will help to give you more information as to what is going on at the site and how you will be accommodated at the site. You can reiterate the questions you have asked the campus placement coordinator and the faculty advisor on topics such as specifying the duties, skills, and hours that will be required. The discussions you have had with the others will help you to be well prepared for the interviews with the site supervisors. Previous discussions will also help you to have focus and to be clear on what your objectives are. Other questions can revolve around the needs of the clients at the site and, more specifically, how those needs are met. Try to ask as many questions as you can. For instance, if you are going to a homeless shelter, you might ask if it offers overnight accommodations, counseling, or only meals. Does it have requirements for its clients such as a particular age or economic status?

The service-learner may also consider being prepared with questions on specific details related to the site such as what type of site is it, is there a training session available, or is it "on-the-job training," and who will be your supervisor? Information regarding training is helpful because agencies can have varying expectations for students, and this interview will give you a better sense of what it is exactly that you will be expected to know. When you contact these organizations directly, express what you have to offer the site members, and be clear about what it is you want to do as a service-learning project. There is also a possibility that you will have to fill out an application as part of the initial meeting. The site supervisor may have to seek out references in order to determine your suitability for the site.

You should feel comfortable that after you have done such a thorough job of recognizing what you need at a service-learning site, as well as what the site supervisor wants, that you are comfortable with the answers you have received from this search-and-question period, that you can go forward and enjoy the benefits of your service-learning experience. If, on the other hand, nothing you have heard about really interests you or grabs your attention, you may consider these other alternatives:

- create an outreach directory of contacts for the organization
- gather data and write a report on a topic/need of the group
- write a public service announcement and distribute it to media outlets
- develop a fundraising plan and/or help implement such a plan
- go through appropriate training and become a speaker for the speaker's bureau
- write an article about the group for publication in an outlet that is important to them
- investigate the procedure and help the group become incorporated as a tax-exempt 501(c)(3)
- help link the organization into a coalition of like-minded groups, and create a forum on campus for the organization to disseminate its message
- work on a publicity campaign for an upcoming activity
- help organize a prayer vigil, demonstration, or other nonviolent action
- write a history of the organization or one of its successful campaigns
- establish a lobbying or advocacy network for the group
- be a counselor/advocate for an especially problematic client
- produce a volunteer recruitment packet or training program for the group
- facilitate the group's use of telecommunications technology (e.g., set up and show how to use e-mail, bulletin boards, or appropriate users' groups)
- interview the leaders and/or members to determine their priorities for the group
- help create/undertake a needs assessment of the client population's priorities
- be a support person/assistant for a burned-out staff member
- evaluate a program or initiative of the group and write a report on it
- produce a documentary of the organization
- develop a lesson plan for teaching a new topic/issue and compile the necessary background information
- be a testing agent/auditor for the organization
- start an oral history of the organization
- create a phone tree or rapid response network to facilitate communication on time-urgent matters (Marullo, S. 1996. Community Involvement Seminar Syllabus. In Ender et al. (eds.), p. 58, *Service-Learning and Undergraduate Sociology: Syllabi and Instructional Materials.* Washington, D.C.: The American Sociological Association).

## Tutoring as a Service-Learning Experience

If you are considering a service-learning project which involves tutoring, this type of project can be extremely rewarding. There is a great deal of work which can be anticipated in preparing to teach, and for these types of experiences some students find that structured programs offer immense assistance when it comes to having service-learners tutor. Structured programs to tutor young children and adults are helpful when preparing for these experiences. If your campus is not affiliated with America Reads, or the Junior Achievement program, you can contact them directly by using the website directory at **www.ablongman.com/ servicelearning.**

In one project which focused on tutoring children who were mostly from a different socioeconomic class and race than the service-learners, the learners reported surprise when they met students who did not fit the stereotypes they had envisioned (Cohen, 1995). Although the service-learners first reported apprehension at the prospect of tutoring, they soon discovered they were welcome at the site. This feeling of the initial discomfort with the setting dissipated when the service-learners were welcomed by principals and teachers and found a strong sense of attachment to the students. In some cases, the students experienced for the first time what it was like to be a minority in a particular social setting. One of the findings from this study, the Community Tutoring Project, was that the service-learners were also discovering more about themselves through these experiences. They started to reanalyze their stereotypes and beliefs about social justice, responsibility to the community, and to critically reevaluate mainstream society.

In another study done by a group of undergraduates who were engaged in a participant observation study in the Alhambra School District, the service-learners questioned their own cultural assumptions and began to analyze the social and institutional influences on group differences (Calderon and Farrell, 1996). In this service-learning study sponsored by Pitzer College, students worked in classrooms and reported on the unintended consequences of some of the structural features of the schools such as seating arrangements, study group organizations, and tracking systems. The undergraduates learned a great deal about the complexity of social life, including the interconnected intricacies of cultural values and structural conditions. More specifically, the service-learners were involved in a project which displayed the effects of focusing on cultural differences, how it can lead to blaming the victim, as well as encouraging ethnic inequality by reinforcing segregation and stereotyping.

The undergraduates in this particular project replace single-causal explanations for educational achievement with more complex analyses of differential patterns. In this way, more is learned about the structural influences on ethnic inequality and how stereotypes are maintained through public schools, even though the educational system is supposed to be rooted in the ideal of equal educational opportunity for all.

Training offers exciting prospects to service-learners because it allows them the opportunity to directly service children in a unique way. The service-learner is offered the opportunity to experience how educational opportunities can be limiting in different situations, and to further explore some of their own preconceptions about others. There is a certain reanalysis and reevaluation that can happen which allows for a broader understanding of complex issues.

## Self-Inventory: Know Your Strengths, Weaknesses, Likes, and Dislikes

If the student finds a particular service-learning site appealing, it can improve the overall quality of the work the student produces because s/he will be involved many hours at the site and will need the ability to feel comfortable working with diverse groups of people. It could therefore be helpful to have some idea of what type of project the service-learner is interested in before beginning the service-learning site visits. Taking the time to carefully assess what type of project would be best for you, and would meet your expectations of what it means to be involved in service-learning, cannot be emphasized.

Completing this section of the guidebook will assist you to get a better sense of what type of project will hold your interest for the time period of the service-learning project. There are also a number of different questions you can ask yourself during the project, but one question can be the focal point: What do you find interesting about this project? What is it that intrigues you and makes it an area you would like to find out more about? The focal point questions can be asked repeatedly so that you can be assessing the situations, the projects, and your own motivations. It can orient you to the important nuances of the project. This may also be a question for the site supervisors—what is it that brings them to do this type of work? What are their motivations? If you were to ask supervisors this might help to determine if your interests are similar.

These questions are a good start to target a good fit between the student and the right site:

### *Student Interest Inventory Worksheet:*
1. What kinds of issues are you most interested in discussing? What do you like to read about?
2. What is your history of work, work-study, volunteer work, or involvement in public issues?
3. What kinds of academic courses are you interested in?
4. What are some of the issues or problems on your campus or in your local community, at school or at home, that concern you?
5. What are your hobbies or special skills?
6. What particular academic skills do you have or are you developing?

Watters and Ford, *A Guide for Change: Resources for Implementing Community Service,* 1995, McGraw-Hill, pp. 33–34. Material is reproduced with the permission of The McGraw-Hill Companies.

Be honest when addressing these questions. Having an open mind and doing some intensive brainstorming now, before beginning the project, will give you a better sense of what suits your needs, as well as saving you from the time and effort it takes to be in the wrong type of situation for a long period of time. This period of soul-searching can also pay off as part of the self-assessment that takes place when considering one's longer-term career goals, political interests, and subsequent civic endeavors.

The six different questions listed above on interests, history, academic courses, social problems, hobbies, and skills are focused to help the students study what they find appealing and fulfilling. Examination of these topics prior to the commencement of the project will give you a better sense of self and the social world of the service-learning site. As you do more reflection, and keep on focusing on your interests, it will give you an opportunity to write on important issues. Reminding yourself of your motivations and interests will give you more of a chance to write on these issues, and this reflective process can greatly improve the quality of your writing. Self-assessment provides an opportunity to provoke a healthy exchange between service-learning events, and your own presuppositions about what you thought would happen at service-learning sites.

Also seriously consider the amount of time you will need to devote to the project, and the time you have available to give to it. Determining the time commitment will help you to assess if you can meet the demands, or if the time it will take will be too overwhelming. The time requirement of the service-learning should include the different phases of the project, the time it will take to write field notes, complete the final paper, meet with the faculty advisor, and do additional readings. When examining the commitment level of the service-learning project, also include what time is required for other coursework.

The service-learner should consider that there is a broad range of service-learning projects, and they can be established to fulfill many different types of circumstances, meet the needs of various populations, and be structured in a variety of ways. It is helpful to view these projects as occurring at different places along a wide spectrum.

Different types of service-learning projects can occur at one end of the spectrum or the other or anywhere in between. The service-learner may be providing assistance to people through one-on-one interaction, or s/he may be doing research on how to provide the best service to people from behind the scenes. S/he might join a prearranged activity or lead a group activity.

The service-learner can choose between providing direct assistance to the clients or providing an advocacy for the group through organizing various lobbying activities. Service-learners may be involved in structured activities where everything is prearranged, or in unstructured projects in which programs are open-ended and may vary in their organization. You may also be in a situation in which you can see a result in the short-term, or you may not be able to observe the results in your project because the social change involved only occurs in the long term. A period of self-examination will help you to assess where you would like to fit in the spectrum and where you need to be in order to get the most out of your service-learning project.

Being involved in service-learning is an exciting prospect. It is exciting to learn more about yourself and the world around you because you may discover more about certain areas that you have previously anticipated. In this way you can look upon the time period before your project begins as a crucial turning point in your life; at this point in time you can carefully examine your own motivations and beliefs. The next section deals with some important safety issues to consider when engaging in your project.

## Safety

This section outlines some safety hazards and ways to deal with various difficult situations. If you are part of a team or group, keep a surveillance going to make sure different members are faring well. Again, the service-learners will not want to crowd each other, or be next to each other at all times, but will check-in with each other by just touching base throughout the site visit, depending upon the neighborhood and safety precautions present at the site. Check-in may consist of meeting each other during certain periods, perhaps every hour on the hour, to see how you are each doing, and to offer each other advice, encouragement, or whatever type of support or advice that might be helpful. At some site locations there may be metal detectors or police guards available to provide added protection to the site employees and clients.

Service-learners may be in a site location that is unsafe or in an impoverished neighborhood. If that is the case, remember that you can still have a rewarding experience wherever you are. Actually, it is possible that when students are in "bad" neighborhoods doing their service, they feel more of a sense of accomplishment because they were able to complete a project despite its reputation, and they knew they were really offering assistance to those who were in need.

If an organization is located in an unsafe area, or if the clientele are considered high risk, the agency may offer workshops that offer advice on how to deal with difficult situations. Also, there may be some general guidelines that are made clear at the outset of your service. The guidelines may sum up some of the rules of behavior that are expected of volunteers and service-learners that may involve refusing to take part in any types of exchanges that include solicitations for money, alcohol, cigarettes, drugs, or phone numbers. If requests for these types of exchanges are repetitive from clients, the service-learner is usually asked to speak to a site supervisor. If these sites are predominantly male, and the service-learner is female, then she may be dealing with unwanted attention. The best way of thwarting unwanted advances is the same as in any situation: Tell the person s/he is being rude and walk away. The site supervisors may offer suggestions on how to deal more specifically with these types of advances.

Some organizations will offer advice on what to wear and what not to wear. Generally, casual or informal clothes are suitable, such as jeans. For both men and women, it is usually best not to have on costly jewelry, and the service-learner, both male and female, will probably feel more comfortable not wearing anything too revealing. Other safety hazards have to deal with transportation difficulties. There might be a vehicle available for service-learning such as a van, bus, or car from the college. If you are the driver, be careful, and try not to drive dangerously at any time. Take a count of service-learners upon entering and leaving to make sure you are departing with the whole group. Sometimes it is difficult to drive a van or bus if you are acclimated to cars. You might want to do a practice drive to get adjusted to it. It is also challenging to find places you may not have been before. Make sure you have good directions by trying out the directions ahead of time and also ask a passenger to help you by giving the directions as you drive, to avoid driving and reading at the same time. Delay conversations on cell phones when driving.

The potential service-learner probably has a better sense now of what activity to engage in, and how to find a placement, while avoiding certain safety hazards. Let us move on to a more detailed description of helpful skills for the service-learner.

# 5 Helpful Skills for the Service-Learner

This section outlines some techniques to use to get the most out of the service-learning experience. These points have been developed based on interviews with students, and students' papers on the topic, which were analyzed to discover what skills are helpful at the service-learning site. As a troubleshooting guide this section can prepare you in advance if you should run into any difficulties while on site.

As stated in the section on finding a placement, you need to do as much homework as you can before you go to the site. Try to clarify with the placement center, or the site members themselves, what your responsibilities will be and how you will be trained for the position. If these expectations are clarified, this will help to make the entire process go much more smoothly. Also make sure you are knowledgeable on the deadlines that the faculty advisor has for you, and the times and places of the site visits so that you can meet those terms. Also ask the professor how your performance will be evaluated so you know what to focus on at the site and in your writing.

If you are feeling nervous about the service-learning and are also intimidated by professors, it is usually possible to locate other students who have experience doing service-learning. They know what you are going through, and have been there before, so they can offer you good advice. You might be able to discover students who have experience by asking the professor for names, e-mail addresses, or phone numbers of past students who are still on campus. More structured Service-Learning Centers on campuses may have CWPs or Community Work Program students who are involved in a government program and usually have extensive experience in the field.

It is also essential to clarify with the other team members (if you are going with a team) what their responsibilities will be, and how it will be necessary for everyone to contribute for the project to be completed. Clarify with the other team members how a high commitment level is essential for the whole project to be considered successful.

The students need to be responsible for their service-learning project. There are site members and clients that are counting on you to be there at certain times and certain dates. If you are not there, the site supervisors will be left to scramble in order to fill the gap, and this can make life more difficult for the site clients. If the students do not show up for assignments, then the college can get an "irresponsible" reputation also. If service-learners do not carry through on responsibilities, disconnection can be the result rather than improved networking.

In addition to following through, another essential skill you can learn in this project is how to gain rapport. Learning how to fit into the scene, and changing your status from outsider to insider, takes time and much effort on your part. It also takes work for the site members because they will need to take the time to get to know and trust you. Certainly, the more visits you make to the site, and the more hours you spend there, can increase the insight you have on the site immensely. Be patient, because entrance, as well as acceptance, is not always easily gained but is very much worth acquiring.

Gaining acceptance is more difficult when the person has a lack of confidence. When students first walk into the social service agency, they may feel that they do not know what to say, the way to act, and even what to wear. Actually, more accurately stated, there may be some trepidation about the project before the student walks in the door. In group situations that uneasiness can be relieved by clinging on to other group members and staying as close together as possible. Unfortunately, that is the wrong impulse to follow because if the student freezes and stays with his or her own group, it is more difficult to make acquaintances, hinders interaction with the clients at the site, decreases the likelihood of learning more about the organization, and influences the way that the entire group will be perceived. We can actually call this staying together as a group the "clumping factor." In fact, some site clients may think that the students do not wish to interact with them, and that students only wish to stay within their own groups. This clumping factor does little to combat the sense of outsider status the student is already feeling when s/he enters the scene, or the outsider status the site client may feel.

It may seem difficult, but the best bit of advice is to separate from the other group members if you have gone to the site with others. It will be more conducive to fitting in, and being perceived as part of the whole scene, and not being someone who is hiding with her or his own "in-group." It will be more likely for you to have face-to-face interaction if you have separated from other members of the group, and this type of interaction can be one of the most enjoyable aspects of the project.

After you have successfully avoided only staying within your own group, the next suggestion I have is to try to do something immediately that helps you to fit into the site. It may be having a meal with clients at a homeless shelter, or playing a game with a group of elderly people in a nursing home. By fitting into the site, rather than standing around on the sidelines, you will feel more comfortable immediately. Try to be as natural as possible, and look upon the social setting as any other social event, a place where you are going into, but are not quite sure what is going on yet, or what is expected of you. In many cases, the clients will know in advance who you are and why you are there, so it is likely you will be looked upon as people who have come to help and assist them in some way. Therefore, you are not going to be looked upon as an enemy, or a person that is going to give them a hard time. They are likely to be looking forward to seeing you and making your acquaintance.

If you do not feel welcome at the site, you must realize this can also happen in a social setting where people do not know who you are. This lack of belongingness can happen anywhere, and there can be a myriad of reasons for it, but you need not take it personally because it is a public area where no one is likely to know you. You also have to reflect on this sense of isolation you can be feeling and wonder how much of it is based on your own fear of the setting, and the preconceived notions you may have of the clients. It is possible that you are so convinced of not being able to fit in that you have brought that

notion to the setting with you. It may be impossible to enter the setting without any preconceived notions, but it is definitely possible to try to gain acceptance from site members, and
to look upon it as any other social setting. Also, the service-learners may be trying to come
to an understanding of how they are being viewed by the clients or how the clients may
have preconceived notions of who the service-learners are. Most likely, the way they view
you is more favorable than the way you think you are being viewed.

Try to focus on the fact that the people you are visiting at the site are not there to
harm you. Some may be people who have faced difficulties in life, whether it was a natural
disaster, a fire, they may be victims of abuse, or they might have lost their jobs, their families, and have no surviving relatives. They are likely to be victims of certain unanticipated
consequences, and they could just as easily be you. Further, some clients might wait until
you have gone to the site again before they start to feel comfortable talking with you. Even
if some clients do not wish to interact, it is still likely you will meet individuals who will
introduce themselves, want to discover more about you, and feel comfortable having a conversation with you.

The best attitude to take upon entering the site is to treat it as you would any other
social setting. You should look upon it as another adventure in life and keep a positive outlook. Try to avoid having stereotypes about categories of people; you cannot predict someone's actions because you think s/he is supposed to act in a certain way. Try to keep calm.

One way to begin interacting with site members and clients is to try to find a connection. Try to start a conversation about anything in particular that can be relatively trivial.
For instance, you can make a comment about the weather, a sport, or current events. Try to
find a common interest which you can discuss such as a foreign language, a city or state, a
game or hobby such as chess or cards. If you can find a starting point in your discussions
you can use it as a stepping-stone to other more frequent and involved conversations. Generally, the best rule of thumb is to keep the conversations as light as possible, without commenting on intrusive topics such as your life history or theirs. If someone is trying to tell
you about their life circumstances, then the best you can do is listen, but do not ask them
serious questions such as Why are you homeless? Or why are you here? These are very private matters and should be discussed only if the person wants to share them with you.

Remember that it is possible that the site members are overworked and may ask you
to take on responsibilities that were not previously negotiated. You may be asked to do
odd jobs such as mopping floors, filing, or shelving items. Be clear about your duties
from the outset, service usually involves some form of direct assistance to clients that involves some form of interaction rather than cleaning jobs. Of course, different circumstances may come up which involves cleaning or straightening up, but it should not be
your only task. You are in a vulnerable position because you do want to help and be of
assistance while also gaining acceptance. The best remedy if you do not feel as though
you are doing what you should be doing, or what was previously arranged, is to discuss
these tasks with someone in charge; it may also help to first outline the problem to someone at the campus placement center, or to your faculty advisor, so they can give you
advice on what exactly should be said and done. When discussing the tasks at the site, you
might mention that there is an assignment attached to your service-learning so that you
must learn from the setting and apply it to the course in order to pass. Usually site supervisors can quickly identify with being able to complete an assignment with a deadline. If

you want an objective opinion, contact your faculty advisor first, before communicating difficulties with the site supervisor.

It is possible that you will be enjoying your service-learning project, that the site supervisors are pleased with your service, and you may be asked to take on more responsibilities quickly. Make sure you can schedule the increased responsibilities into your daily class, work, or leisure time activities. If you take on too many responsibilities quickly, particularly if you are assuming more of a leadership or supervisory role, you may find that all of the transitions made in a short period of time can be difficult to cope with and may add undue stress to the situation. One step at a time is good advice to take to avoid an overload. The goal is to enjoy the service-learning project without experiencing burnout.

There may also be some difficulties in areas that you would not anticipate as causing trouble. Students can find the details involved in organizing and arranging site visits difficult to expedite. There are invariably scheduling snafus, difficulties when making appointments to deal with everyone's busy schedules, or problems with transportation. If the details are overwhelming it is helpful to discuss these issues with someone who is familiar with the organization or someone who has done the same type of service-learning in the past. Again, those who have crossed these paths before can offer invaluable advice.

How you feel about yourself tends to affect the research that you are involved in, including how you relate to others, and how you react to particular circumstances. You may begin the project with excitement, and some fear, but later you may experience disillusionment or maybe even dislike for the setting. You may meet hostile people, or you may be in situations which can be considered conflictual. If that does happen, remember it may be uncomfortable, but it can yield quite a lot of information about the setting and its very political nature that you might not have known previously. Finding out valuable information may be one of the unanticipated consequences of the hostile or conflictual experience. Understanding that you are likely to be affected by the setting will assist you in dealing with these complex emotions. It may be helpful to have other students or professors available to discuss these feelings with, and also recording these feelings and reflecting on them in a journal will assist you in dealing with certain feelings you may be experiencing.

To assist you in recording your experiences in a journal, try to listen and observe. Try to take mental notes of what you see happen, what individuals are doing, and be as descriptive as possible. Even relatively small events can be emblematic of larger trends; in other words, even something which might be regarded as trivial can mean a great deal when analyzed as a part of the larger context. It makes sense to take note of how individuals behave and what they say or do, because these details can lead to clues about the organization and about the larger social world. Observational skills are important at the scene. When you watch others you can observe so much such as what everyone wears, how they act, facial expressions, postures, etc. Also, observing takes your mind off yourself and how you feel. Interviewing skills are also important. Try to ask questions of the site supervisors such as how long have they worked there, what makes their jobs worthwhile, how long has the facility been opened. Try not to interrupt or to be thinking of your next question but listen intently to what people are saying.

Listening is key to discovering more about any social situation. Another key is writing. Remember that writing is thinking. You will find that as you write, more and more thoughts that you had and events that occurred can come flooding back to you. Try to write field notes on the site visits, being as detailed as possible, as soon as possible after the visit. If possible, you might consider writing them directly after the site visit, on the trip back to campus. The longer you wait after the visit, the more memories you will lose. Directly after the visit, you will have more recollection than at any other time. The day after you will have lost at least half of the details. This point cannot be over-emphasized.

At this point, the service-learner may feel inundated with dos and don'ts of getting involved in these types of projects. It may be difficult to remember all of these tips at once, and it is therefore important to say that it is very tough to keep track of every different right and wrong—it is also impossible to avoid making mistakes. The true intent of this section is to do some troubleshooting so that you will not feel like a stranger at the service-learning site, and that you will have some advice to rely on if necessary. Even if you do feel awkward at the site, and do things you might have wished you did not do, you will not feel that way for long. There is much solace to be gained by realizing that others have attempted these types of projects before, and may have made mistakes at times, but concluded the project successfully, knowing more about themselves, while they reached out to others in ways that were incomprehensible to them at the inception of the project, but are part of their reality now. It will probably be part of your reality soon to know that you, too, have made a difference. The next chapter is dedicated to helping the service-learner achieve this goal by carefully outlining how to do field research.

# 6 Tips on Doing Field Research: A How-To Guide on Participant Observation

This section is dedicated to the discussion of participant observation and includes a how-to guide on what to pay attention to when involved at the site, including how to use your senses to do field research and how to maintain a sense of curiosity about the setting. This part of the manual offers the service-learner general guidelines on how to do participant observation, but is only a guide, and ultimately it is your decision what to do at a site, and what is the single best course of action in different situations. In order to properly deal with certain circumstances, you may find that you use your own common sense, as well as advice from your faculty advisor, site supervisors, and clients.

One important guideline is to try to pay attention to what is going on in different settings in order to write about your site visits thoroughly. Even slight details that may not seem important can become more significant when you find out more about the site. For instance, you might take note that someone always sits in the same seat, but you may find out after a few visits that there is a reason for that particular seating arrangement. Observe how people are interacting and acting, the way they speak to one another and yourself, and of course, take note of what are important conversation topics. Usually, so many events are happening simultaneously that it may be difficult to figure out what to focus on exactly. It is helpful to consider using your senses in order to pinpoint the different events that are making impressions on you. In that way you can include these impressions in your field notes. Use the sights, sounds, and the way food tastes to make an impression on you, so that you can reflect on them when you leave the site.

Paying attention to what you first observe using your senses is helpful in a number of ways. First, the outsiders who first enter a scene can notice things that the insiders, or the frequent visitors, do not notice. This may be because they are used to these occurrences or are not noticing them anymore. Second, the researcher will want to maintain this "culture shock," or this feeling of newness, in order to keep a sense of curiosity and wonder about the site. The feeling of curiosity, and seeing things for the first time, can be renewed by visiting other sites. If you visit other places, and then return to the original site, it will help you to notice features of the setting by comparison, which may have escaped your notice previously. Visiting other sites will help you to remain curious about the site.

Third, the researcher can constantly ask questions about the site, and be interpreting the events continuously, particularly paying attention to moments when s/he is shocked, or surprised, or disappointed. By asking yourself questions, you can maintain a sense of wonder about what is going on at the site. Asking yourself questions allows you to reflect on the experiences also.

You may be wondering what to pay attention to, and what to write about in your field notes. At the beginning of the project, you should see yourself as a novice who is curious and has wonder and excitement about where you are. It is helpful to see yourself as a learner. As a learner it is important to watch, and take note of those things you see, and not to be concerned at the outset about issues such as categorizing, application of theory, etc. It is helpful to pay attention to people: What are they wearing, how do they act, and how many there are? Also essential is to take in the physical setting: What is in the space, how is it set up, what are the sounds? Also the researcher can take notes on the events or activities of the site: What is being done, are people engaging in conversations with others, are they alone, or do they participate in teams (Schatzman and Strauss, 1973)?

When you are involved in writing down what your senses are taking in, it is up to you to determine if you should sit, stand, move around, or converse, and you may try all of these to determine which is most comfortable. The important point is to note the details that you can. It may not even seem inappropriate to take notes in front of people, and you may prefer writing on your own after the site visit. When you do write, just try to avoid being general and vague about the scene and focus instead on describing exactly what you see as much as possible. Try writing about individuals, rather than groups; if you describe an individual it will encourage more detail than describing a group of people.

Your senses will be taking in a lot of information all at once while engaged in service-learning. Therefore, while the service-learner observes, s/he is also listening and making sense of verbal clues. Your observations will be augmented by asking questions, and listening to the answers. By taking notes and listening, your research becomes more sophisticated as you write more field notes for each visit, and you continue to make visits.

While taking notes, and observing, and participating in certain duties, you may notice that your presence in the interaction is causing people to behave differently than they would normally. This may actually raise questions for you as to whether or not you are writing about something that happens on a routine basis, or some occurrence which is taking place because you are present, and participating in the goings-on at the site. This reaction of people to the presence of the researcher is called "reactivity," and although it may cause you to wonder about the reliability of your notes to capture the daily routine of the site, it is still helpful to be present and take note of even how you might feel you are impacting the daily routine of the service-learning site. You may write about whether or not you think your presence causes disruption, and if that reactivity changes as you become more of an insider at the site and make more regular visits.

Most service-learners do not want their presence to cause unnecessary disruption to the site, but if it does happen, it can be studied as a part of the project. For example, one day we visited a site that I had visited with previous classes. It was a facility that served meals to clients who were homeless. When we entered for the first time that semester we sat in on an orientation with the director of the facility. He said that they also had elected a group of site clients to represent the opinions of the site clientele. One of the elected site clients spoke to our group, telling us that they felt that we had in the past asked intrusive questions which made the clients feel like they were in a fishbowl and that they did not always like being asked why they were homeless, for instance. The speaker cautioned us against asking intrusive questions. While I think that this was meant as merely a caution, and not to preclude us from visiting, the students felt as though their presence at the site was so intrusive that they told me they did not feel comfortable. Nevertheless, we had made a time commitment, and the project was completed. The orientation of the site members became a discussion topic among the students and stirred up some awkward feelings. Students have reported in their papers feeling very anxious at the time of arrival to the site, and this event aggravated an already unpleasant feeling of not being welcomed.

For this class, we decided to make the orientation the clients gave us as a way of discovering more about the site, so we as a class were able to discuss why we thought the site members felt as they did, and these discussions promoted good reflective writing. Therefore, the orientation became a key part of the study. Students wrote about how they felt their presence at the site aggravated the client's sense of being labeled, and stigmatized. Also, other site members made a point of telling us that the orientation comments were made by a very small minority at the shelter and that most of its members really looked forward to spending time with them, interacting with them, and sharing meals with them.

Turning difficulties at the setting into positive circumstances is one of the best ways to deal with field research. In the case of this particular class, we were causing a change in the normal day-to-day events at the site, and we made the best of it by making the change an integral section of the field research. In this way, a problem was turned into data. One of the risks of being a known researcher in a situation is the risk of changing the situation from what it would have been without you present, but this is also an advantage in that you will be allowed to find out more about the context of the site than you would have if you had remained an outsider. In that class, we were able to see firsthand what it was like to be a participant observer.

At the site, being actively engaged in a service-learning project, the researcher will be taking on the status of participant observer. Participant observers are involved in ongoing activities, and at the same time, can have a known identity as a researcher. For the general purposes of service-learning, most students are known to be involved in the projects for course credit, and people at the site are aware that students are actively engaged in studying the site. This is an important distinction to make because there are cases in which researchers enter scenes secretly, and do not make their presence known as researchers. Reactivity is more of an issue when the presence of a researcher is known because the clients may change their normal everyday interaction.

It will be helpful to outline some of the rewards and drawbacks of participant observation as a strategy in service-learning. One disadvantage is that you may be so busy doing a certain type of work in a specific area that you are not able to be curious and learn about other activities at the service-learning site. You may learn a great deal about what goes on in one part of the place and not have a holistic view of the entire site. There may be services that the organization provides that you remain unaware of because you have been absorbed in another practice the site engages in. For example, you may work in assisting site supervisors in a child-care capacity, but not be involved in the food-service program the organization also provides. The disadvantage, then, is that you do not get a sense of the entire operation. This of course, can be turned into an advantage if you perceive it in that way, because the one area you do participate in you do know very well before you leave the site.

Another possible deficit is that the student may "go native," or "become the phenomenon" as you are participating in the scene, and you are an active part of what goes on. You may take on a particular point of view of its members, and become so involved that you cannot see other perspectives (Jorgenson, 1989). This is another reason why it would be helpful to visit other sites that are also involved in the same type of community involvement. If you have time, it can broaden your insight considerably to participate in other programs and see if the clients there have similar perspectives.

A distinct advantage to participant observation is that you are gaining knowledge in areas that outsiders might not be allowed to delve into or might not be able to find out at all. The participant observer can see what happens, and will be allowed to discover more about certain situations than would a casual visitor. It is also possible that the researcher will find out what it is like to be working at the site by sharing the daily surprises, worries, and accomplishments with the site supervisors.

Participant observation is a good method to discover more about the clients' and the site supervisors' everyday perspectives. The service-learner can discover the meanings people (both clients and supervisors) have for events in their lives, and how they interact with one another. As the service-learner gets better acquainted with people s/he will be allowed greater access into all kinds of interactions. Participating and observing at the same time gives the service-learner access into the context of the lives of the people at the site. By "context" I am referring to the interactions, the unwritten rules, and the perspectives of the people involved in the project that you discover through time, including those situations people may not always talk about to outsiders.

With time it is possible to learn more about the contextual features of a site, and to become more of an insider, as people have a tendency to involve you more as they begin to trust you. You may be called upon to participate by contributing an expertise, or assist people at the site, and you may be engaged in participant observation as part of a team of researchers. If a team approach is possible, the participants may be able to divide the labor and come up with a variety of perspectives regarding what is going on at the site. The team approach can be an advantage because the results are not only contingent upon one researcher's skills and perspectives, but the others can add their abilities and their interpretations. This process of information sharing can be of great assistance when problem solving and thinking about alternative plans and options. In the group format there can be a discussion among a group of service-learners as to what the different contextual features are of the site that are relevant, and whether or not you agree or disagree on your different interpretations. As a group you can share information and insights into the goings-on at the site.

Whether you are involved in service-learning alone, or as a part of a team, the service-learner as participant observer is getting to experience the situational context at the site more than s/he would have if s/he would have remained an outsider. An outsider in this description is one who observes situations from afar without including himself or herself on the scene. If you do use your senses to take in the different stimuli around you, you can learn an enormous amount about the goings-on at the community-based organization and, at the same time, learn a tremendous amount of information about yourself. Next, we will turn to a discussion of how to gain acceptance at the site.

# Gaining Acceptance

An initial concern when entering the site is to gain acceptance, to be sure that the insiders would like to have you present. The best way to do this is to blend in with the scene as much as possible and not to do anything that calls undue attention to you. In order to do this listen to what is being said and going on in the setting in order to determine how members act and dress. If anyone asks you questions about what your purposes are in the setting, and your reasons for being there, you should answer them directly and openly. Some insiders might regard you as a valuable person to maintain a relationship with, and others may view you with suspicion. All you need to do is to be candid about your service-learning project and to be brief. If anyone wants details, s/he will ask you directly.

Insiders may need assurance that they will not be harmed by your study. If they ask about the project it would be helpful to explain that their participation in the study is voluntary, that their identity will be kept anonymous, and that the information they give you will be kept confidential. This assurance may help because not everyone will want their thoughts and feelings to be made public. Being made aware of confidentiality can be very much a relief to someone who is considering discussing his or her personal life with you. This process of gaining acceptance may take some time, particularly if you are in a setting where people are feeling vulnerable. It is important only to understand this and realize that some will have an easier time developing a relationship with you than others, just as in any social circumstances.

Developing relationships with the people at the site is similar to developing any kind of friendship. People are looking for others who are open-minded and not quick to judge their situations. They are also looking for compassionate, sympathetic people who are willing to take the time to listen to them. Therefore, try to remember what people say to you, and next time you see them, follow up with how they are doing, or bring up something they discussed with you again. Remembering what they have confided in you can go a long way toward establishing rapport. Also, as in any relationship, try to be sincere. People can usually spot duplicity quickly. Truth about oneself is going to be a key factor in getting to fit in and become acquainted with others.

Gaining rapport through participant observation means that by participating at the site you have shared experiences with the site participants, and you are engaged in more of the same activities. Sharing experiences helps to build bonds and soften the boundaries that may exist between the insider and the outsider. This allows for a solidarity, and a sense of camaraderie, or a "we" feeling.

It is important when engaged in participant observation to keep focus on how the members themselves account for what is going on at the site. It is important to be able to take the role of the other, or understand how the site members make sense of the site and their places in it. This is not only important for the site clientele but is also helpful to know more about the site supervisors. At the beginning of the project, it is important to understand the individual's perspective, without relying on your own framework for understanding. This may be easier to write about than to actually do, because you will have to take your own preconceptions about life and "suspend" them, or put them aside. Instead, try to get a handle on how the person you are talking to deals with life, and how they describe what is important to them. If you can actually put yourself into the role another person plays in life, you have accomplished a great deal in the service-learning project.

## Taking Notes

In some situations, it will be acceptable for the researcher to be taking notes while in a setting. It may not be regarded as suitable in different situations, depending upon the social norms of the encounter. It is usually easy to discern if you are making others uncomfortable by taking notes, if that is the case, then your notes would be increasing reactivity. Another alternative may be to observe, converse with others, and then take notes in another area such as the bathroom, outside, or in a private place you may find at the site. If you can avoid taking notes in front of the people you are working with, it may relieve them from feeling as though they are "on stage." Some people shrink at the idea of being an object of a research project. Others may be impressed with the fact that they can include themselves in a valuable study that discovers more about important topics. It is difficult to tell which person you may be speaking with, one who is open to being included, or one who would rather not be, unless you ask them.

There are also two different types of notes you can write, one is brief and the other is a longer and more descriptive version of what happened at the site. One group of notes can be brief and cursory notes, which include just words and phrases of what you saw or experienced. These brief notes can then be filled in later with full idea development, and a more thorough outline of what actually happened. You may want to avoid only having brief notes that may make no sense at all a few days after the site visit. Longer notes with elaboration should be filled in within a few hours of the brief notes (Schatzman and Strauss, 1973).

Some questions you may wish to answer when writing your notes are questions on the physical space of the setting. How is it set up, what is unusual about it, or is it helpful or not? You may also wish to focus on people at the setting. How they are dressed, how they organize themselves, what are their approximate ages, gender, or ethnicity? Further, what exactly do you see people doing, how do they arrange themselves, is there anything striking about them are all good topics for writing notes. Again, try to be detailed and focus on one individual at a time as you are answering these questions in your notes. As your time at the site increases, you will have more focused observation on individuals that you are participating with in various activities, and you can also ask general, "casual" questions, which are not obtrusive, in order to facilitate conversation and to build relationships. "Casual" questions refer to questions about the weather, sports, current events, food, and other topics such as these.

It also will help to maintain a chronology of events at the site, a running description of what happened, who did what, and an account of events will help when you are analyzing your notes. You may be required to, or have interest in a particular central topic and you may start to concentrate your notes according to that topic. Do not be surprised if you are spending as much time with notes as you are with the actual service-learning. This is plausible and beneficial, because it is writing and analyzing of notes which will allow you to focus on certain topics, arrange your thoughts, organize your activities, and also give you insight into which area should be investigated next.

You may find yourself using your memory more and more as you get involved in your service-learning project, you may get better with time about remembering specific details for your field notes. Even the most experienced researchers, though, will lose the specific details of their observational activities after a day or two after the experience. You may decide to write brief notes first, directly after the site visit, and then do something else before filling in the details. When you have decided to fill in your notes with greater detail, remember to transport yourself mentally back to the scene in order to detail your trip to the site. Try to visualize being there again, and the chain of events which transpired.

It will also be helpful to include your feelings in your notes. Discuss how you felt, what you enjoyed, your successes and excitement, but also include your disappointments and frustrations. This can assist you in terms of expressing yourself, and may also indicate future courses of actions. For example, if you were upset that you did not meet someone, writing about it can remind you to make certain you try to meet him or her the next time, or it will remind you to make an effort to interact with as many people, clients, and site supervisors as you can the next time you visit the site. Outline your hunches, intuitions or inclinations about certain events, as they may also prove to be valuable in determining what to look for next, and what area to pay special attention to.

To provide you with some guidelines, here is an example of field notes from a service-learner, and I will also indicate for you what essential elements make these notes unique:

> When I was first made aware of the fact that I was going to have to take part in a service-learning project I had mixed feelings on the assignment. When I heard some of the different types of locations we may be assigned to I was not very excited. I like helping people but I guess I wasn't thrilled about going to feed the poor, because I had done that in the past and I felt absolutely horrible for the people, they looked so miserable. I did not want to go through something like that again. But when I heard there was a chance that I might be able to play with some kids I was excited about that…I was relieved when I found out that I was going to work with the children, I was even excited. These visits were weeks away, so for awhile I was just excited to go. I love working with children, so I felt that this would be a worthwhile experience for me…
>
> But as the date came closer and I learned more about the site and what I was supposed to do some other factors came to mind that I had not considered. When I found that the kids were going to be at the homeless shelter what came to mind was that the children would be less fortunate than the kids I was used to playing with. That was not a problem to me, because a kid is a kid, they all have feelings, all laugh, and all smile, so I was still excited to play with the children. But the only thing I was concerned about is that usually children who come from less fortunate homes are not as clean. I knew this was a stereotype and not always true, but my mom is a school nurse at an elementary school and she comes across this on a daily basis. When working with little kids, in past experiences they always become attached, especially older children, and they cling to you. I was scared that I would have to be careful of how close I got to the children in case one of them had lice or something. The only other problem is that I am an emotional person and that if the children seemed as though they were from really poor situations I would feel incredibly bad for them (Paul, undergraduate student, freshman year).

This particular set of field notes is excellent because the writer included important feelings that reflected some ambivalence about the site visits. These notes are descriptive, detailed, and they convey some feelings, concerns, and anxieties before entering the site. They also indicate to the reader a sense of how ideas about upcoming events can change as time passes. These notes in particular are so detailed that the reader can get the sense that the student is reliving their experiences prior to the event, and also being very honest about them. It is also important to note that the feelings themselves are not the basis for the "A" grade the student received. The writing does not necessarily have to convey excitement about the project in order to be evaluated well. The students can also receive a good grade if they write about dreading the assignment, and if they are experiencing feelings of frustration, or a total lack of enthusiasm. Detail and honesty are two factors which make for a good grade. Therefore, what is important is *how* you express what you are feeling, rather than *what* you are feeling.

# Interviewing

A service-learning assignment may require interviewing the clients at a particular community-based organization in order to discover more about them. In cases where interviewing is required for the service-learning project, always make sure to tell the interviewee that s/he has a right to skip certain questions if s/he does not choose to discuss them at all. The interviewee needs only to tell you "skip it," and it will not be considered part of the interview. Also, if the interviewer would like you to turn off the tape recorder at any point, or not to tape the interview at all, they need only tell you. Prior to the interview, you may ask for their permission to interview them, and set up a time, but be certain to confirm with them that their identities will be kept confidential, and that they will have the right to tell you when they do not wish to answer a question.

The service-learner may be asked to complete informal interviews, formal interviews, in-depth interviews, or life histories. In informal interviews the questions are general, the answers can be free-flowing, and can assume the pace of a natural conversation. The difference between casual questioning and an informal interview is usually that in an informal interview, the interviewer will either take notes on the answers to questions, or, with the client's permission, tape the discussion. Informal and formal interviews differ in that in an informal interview questions are general and open-ended, meaning they can lead to other topics. Formal interviews are usually more precise and include questions that are more precise, and the interviewer might lead the interviewee back to certain questions as they are the focus and structure of the interview.

An in-depth interview generally focuses on discussion with one person who is very knowledgeable in a particular field that you are studying, and the interview can last for up to 3 hours. The in-depth interview is generally conducted over a period of time, and the interviewee may be asked to be interviewed over a period of weeks, months, or years on a regular basis. In-depth interviews may be required in order to ask general questions about a particular topic to help the service-learner with a perplexing problem or inconsistency encountered. In-depth interviewing is generally done with an individual who has been a key informant in a comprehensive study of different topics and can include such experts as an inventor, a physician, or a drug smuggler. If the in-depth interview is extended it can also become a life history that would include an extensive description of the life of a key insider.

For any one of these different areas, the faculty advisor can give you a complete guideline of what specific questions can be asked on an interview as is required for the course. There may also be suggestions for how to conduct the interview as well as guidelines for what particular topics should be covered.

The different types of interviews that you may be conducting will require that you write about them in ways that vary, depending upon the requirements of the course. But there are some basic strategies that you can use to translate the experiences into words for the purposes of writing a really good paper. These will be discussed in the next section.

# Writing about your experiences

Even if it is not required in the course, writing journal entries allows you to engage in a written form of reflection. However, reflection can take several other forms, such as discussing the experiences with others or engaging in group exercises regarding your project. Service-learners can get together as a group to discuss the service-learning project in order to openly reflect on what is going on at the site. This can involve getting other people's perspectives on what site supervisors do, and how clients interact with the site supervisors. If there are other people in your class who are actively engaged in service-learning, discussing the site visits may help you in order to express what you have been experiencing, and get the sense of what you may need to pay attention to when you visit next, or when you write your paper. It is also possible your faculty advisor will give you group exercises created to help the group collectively reflect on the service-learning project. The danger involved in group reflection is that, as you start to share the thoughts and feelings of others, you take on their ideas. This is not an intentional act of assuming other people's perspectives but may be an indirect result of sharing insights.

The importance of reflection cannot be overstated because it is through reflection that the examination of the project is done and may be shared with others, which is one of the major goals of service-learning. Through reflection, students can learn about the complexities involved in different social problems. Students can also learn more about reframing questions related to the service-learning, and to take a whole new look at some causes of different social phenomena. For example, service-learners may notice that important questions may be asked on local, state, or federal levels. If homelessness is the topic of the service-learning project, and service-learners are trying to determine the causes of homelessness, they might look to trends in a particular locality, at different time periods, to figure out if homelessness has been on the rise, or steadily decreasing and then try to reflect on some reasons for the changes. Reflection can help lead to a more comprehensive understanding of the project, and gives the student a deeper insight into the conditions surrounding these important social issues.

Even if it is not a requirement for the course you are taking, writing in a journal can help you conceptualize and analyze your service-learning experiences. After each service-learning visit, you should write down detailed field notes that describe your visits, including what you observed in the setting and the specific verbal and nonverbal clues you notice at the site. By offering a chronological and detailed report, you will have a journal that unfolds the experiences before your eyes, and indicates how your perspectives have changed after every visit, and how you may be changing and adapting to the situations, which have occurred. Because the purpose of the journal is to be reflective, one of the key topics in your writing is yourself. You may also discover that by writing in a journal you are evaluating your project as a part of an ongoing process and giving it a written form of assessment. Journal writing may give you ideas on what to do next, or how to approach the next site visit.

Try to be honest in your notes and write down your prior thoughts and feelings before you go to the site, and then write down what actually happened on that site visit, including your thoughts and impressions afterwards. This process of reflection is a key part of the service-learning project because you will be observing the changes in your own life that may be a result of the site visits and also be noticing different things about the site. Writing is helpful to reflect, because you will be able to analyze your prior thoughts, while making comparisons between your thoughts after the events. By maintaining these notes throughout your field research, you will have compiled interesting comparative analyses of your thought-and-action sequences.

In the written assignments for courses that focus on service-learning there is usually a theme involved, whether it is inequality, social stratification, poverty, educational opportunity, etc. Keep in mind as you are engaging in the service-learning, how that theme connects to your service. In most cases faculty advisors will want to see relationships between the service-learning and the course. Try to cite as many examples in writing as possible that demonstrate course concepts, readings, lectures, or class discussions. The connections between the course and the service-learning are important in the reflective process, and should be done throughout the course, rather than at the end only. As the course progresses, try to analyze how the content of the course can be applied to your service-learning site visits.

Connecting the course concepts to the service-learning is an integral feature in the process, and can be time-consuming if you do not have that much experience in this type of application. You may consider discussing the project with other members of your group, your classmates, or your faculty advisor in order to brainstorm on connecting the service to the course concepts. At times discussing the topic with others is like writing about it, as you discuss it, you can get a whole new interpretation. Faculty advisors are also usually willing to read drafts and offer you advice on application of course principles, they may also have copies of past papers in which students were able to write well on their service-learning projects. Other students who have taken the class before may be willing to also read drafts of your paper and offer advice and assistance. Some classes require "journal sharing" in which students are evaluating each others' papers, and giving advice to one another. This can be very helpful in terms of getting insight into what an objective person thinks of your paper, and also reading what others are getting from the project. However, there is also a danger similar to the challenge of reflecting in a group, that you include others' ideas into your reports just from having shared journal entries with them.

The faculty advisor can also help you to think about your service-learning, and the area you are studying, in different ways than you previously conceived of it. For instance, if you had stereotypical ideas of welfare recipients, you may change your preconceptions. The professor may pose questions on the topics, and propose unfamiliar hypotheses that you had not previously considered. In this way you are learning to develop alternative explanations for certain social problems and you may very well start to question your original perceptions of certain social issues. You may also be challenged to reflect on your own social worlds, and to think about how they differ from those of the agency's clients (Blau, Judith, 1999). The reflective process can therefore be guided in ways that will allow you a more comprehensive and broadened perspective.

Again, make sure that you guarantee the site clients' anonymity and confidentiality in your writing. This provides the clients with confidence in knowing that their own personal comments and life histories will be kept out of the public eye. Even if the only reader of your paper is your professor, it is still a basic right that individuals have to their own private lives. It is also helpful to find out if the faculty advisor is planning on giving your journals to other site members, or to the service-learning center, after you have handed it in. If so, this puts the client's comments under increased inspection because the site that has been housing, feeding, or taking care of him or her may then have some information on the client which s/he would have preferred others *did not know.* It would not be unreasonable to anticipate that a site supervisor could read that a particular client found something about the site unhelpful or that s/he dislikes someone who works there. This information which is based on a written report to you could then be used against the client. It could possibly increase conflict between a client and a site supervisor and may even turn into a client losing services, or being reprimanded, or being asked to leave the site. The important point to remember is that if the client divulged certain information to you, they also trusted you with that communication, which should not go further. Trust is key to having a good interaction with another person, as in any relationship, you should be able to confide in one another without repercussions.

You may still not know what to write about for your project exactly so this section includes some provocative and thought-provoking questions developed about service-learning which may help to motivate you to write about the service-learning experiences:

- Who benefits from what this organization does? Is anyone harmed by its efforts? How and why?
- Why are people involved in this work?
- What are the causes and consequences of the problem that this agency/organization addresses? How could/should this problem be addressed differently?
- What structural changes would have to take place to help alleviate this problem? How might such changes be instigated and implemented? What are the barriers to making changes?
- Can one envision a society in which this agency is unnecessary? What would such a society look like? Is it achievable?
- Who has power in the city, in this organization, and in relationships within the organization? How is that power exercised?
- What are the sources and consequences of the inequality of power? How do other forms of social inequality—race, class, gender, age, sexual orientation—bear on the work of this organization and on one's own work within it?

- What is the impact of "service" on the "clients" and on others within the community? (Strand, 1999: 35–36)

Reprinted with permission from "Sociology and Service-Learning: A Critical Look," by Kerry J. Strand, in *Cultivating the Sociological Imagination: Concepts and Models in Service-Learning in Sociology,* James Ostrow, Garry Hesser, and Sandra Enos, volume editors. © 1999 by AAHE. The volume is one of 18 in AAHE's Series on Service-Learning in the Disciplines, Edward Zlotkowski, series editor, published by the American Association for Higher Education, Washington, D.C.

In this section the writing process was discussed as possible either as a solitary or a group process, or both. It can be helpful for the service-learner to reflect on some of the issues encountered in terms of his or her own thoughts, feelings, and preconceptions and to also engage in group discussions on the service-learning project. Also, by engaging in these group discussions, you may have a better sense of how to connect the service-learning to the course. The next section deals with what type of work is involved when you analyze your writings.

## Analyzing the Field Notes

After writing down field notes, it is important to analyze them in order to write a comprehensive paper. When the faculty advisor discusses the "analysis" that is necessary to write a good paper, it is important to know what it means to do "analysis." Analyzing means breaking down the notes into parts and critically reorganizing them in terms of discovering patterns, processes, themes, or topics. You will generally find that it is possible to sort your field notes in terms of parts of a process, or according to a particular category. For instance, you may choose to focus your analysis on the clientele who visit the site, and you may arrange your notes according to when they first enter, receive assistance, get to know others, and exit the process. This categorization would be set up to describe the step-by-step procedure that the client encounters at the site. This is only one way to analyze your notes. It may be up to you how you would like them organized or your faculty advisor may have explicit instructions. Another idea is to organize your notes according to your visit to the service-learning site. Arrange your field notes according to when you first enter, receive training or orientation, start to interact with site supervisors and clients, and return to the site repeatedly. In this way, you would have a chronological description of what you went through at the site, how you were accepted, and eventually how you exited.

As you gather more and more data, as field notes are data, it may be helpful to ask yourself if there is a pattern emerging in your notes. Are there relationships or connections between different events or behaviors, and are those connections part of some larger scheme? Discovering connections or patterns in the data may mean trying to discover if there is a particular event most of the clientele experience? Try to determine if the clients establish similar initiations or interactional relationships with others, with service-learners, or with staff members. It may be interesting to consider comparing and contrasting different persons or events, and trying to sort out similarities or differences. Trying to discern these features by comparison can help you to discover if there is a general typology to describe in the study. For example, you may wish to analyze the differences and the similarities between the mornings at the site and the afternoons or evenings. You may find that at different times of the day the site has unique rhythms. There may be some type of differences between the goings-on at different times, and the site supervisors, and clients may shift their attendance at the site according to particular times of the day. The service-learner can then write about how clients and supervisors alter the site setting. Changing your duties at the site, and also going to other sites in your area that are involved in similar practices, may also help you to discern patterns and themes, which emerge through constant comparison.

Another suggestion for improving analysis is taken from an assignment called the service-learning journal that was based on a course taught by James Ostrow, Ph.D., at Bentley College in Waltham, Massachusetts. The journal, which would be due at the end of the semester, would consist of three parts, field notes, reflection, and a final paper. The first part of the journal is the field notes, which are detailed and chronological reports of what went on at the site, this section also includes how the student felt prior to the site visit and afterwards. General suggestions I would give students were to focus on providing an accurate and detailed report of the happenings at the site, while carefully including your own thoughts and feelings, as you reflect on your experiences before, during, and after site visits. For your field notes, it is best to again include not only your external environment, but also your own internal environment. In your writing of field notes for your journal, describe what you are feeling and thinking about the service-learning visit before you go, while you were there, and what you feel after exiting the location. If you include what you are feeling, in addition to what actually happens around you, you will be well on your way to writing good notes. It may also be of great assistance to read through an excellent example, written before and after site visits by a student in one of my Introduction to Sociology classes:

Here are some excellent field notes that were written before and after the site visits:

Before: As tomorrow is my first visit to the nursing home, I am overcome with a variety of emotions and expectations. I really do not know what to expect and I guess this causes my anxiety. I feel that it is hard for me to relate to older people in general, which causes me to question why I decided to do this 4th credit option to begin with. But I will address my emotion first. Elderly people tend to intimidate me, especially those with diseases or conditions in which I have not been exposed to. I am uncertain of the way I should act or respond to them and this makes me uncomfortable. Those with Alzheimer's are especially hard to communicate with as well as those that don't talk at all. I do not want to cause even more problems for these older people, as they have been through a lot already. But even though my anxiety is causing me to question my decision, I reassure myself that I am doing a good thing—that this experience will help me be a better person, and if at all possible, impact the lives of those I will meet. I know some old people are cranky and mad at the world, but others are genuinely kind and fun to be with. I am looking forward to meeting them. As for my expectations of the day itself, I will arrive at the nursing home and hopefully be introduced to a lot of the elderly, I hope to talk with them and play games and perhaps in the future I will lead group activities. To address the issue of why I am doing this credit option, I really have no idea. When Professor Hamner introduced the idea, I immediately thought it would be fun and decided to do it. But after carefully thinking about it, I decided that I wanted to do this to try to benefit others, maybe bring a smile to someone else's face, if only for an hour. I hope to challenge myself to learn from this experience and to be open and social (Joan, undergraduate student, freshman year).

Joan's field notes are very good due to her insistence on detail and including herself in her notes. She is carefully analyzing her thoughts and feelings about the assignment, and examining them in her notes. This is important because she is focusing on her preconceptions about the assignment, and the people she will meet. These notes are also instructive because they deal with how she is imagining the people she will work with. She describes them as potentially sick, hard to communicate with, cranky, and mad at the world. She outlines how she feels a certain sense of anxiety about the project, based on feeling that she will be an imposition upon the elderly, or cause more problems for them than they need. Joan's notes express an uncertainty about beginning the project, and seem to be questioning her own motives as to why she has gotten herself involved in the service-learning, and then she rationalizes for herself the reasons she did choose to do the 4th credit option, including the way this project will help make her a better person, challenge herself to learn, and help others. Joan's work is expressive in the way she studies her anxiety and the source of her anxiety. Joan's notes are an excellent starting point for post-visit field notes and future analysis.

Joan's notes are also informative as she continues the site visits, and writes before-and-after notes:

> After: I seem to always leave the adult day care center with a quiet satisfaction. I definitely learned more about the elderly, but I had fun too. One of the men called me Lady Godiva today and that made me laugh. They come out with these weird phrases that put a smile on my face. I think most people would not be able to put up with the nonsense that is usually associated with the elderly [me included until I started this work], but now I find it is a relaxing escape from the stress of my life. I went there today with a thousand things on my mind and so many things that needed to be accomplished this week, but I found myself forgetting them while I was there. Though the job is definitely not easy for people that work full-time, I find it enjoyable as of now. I have one more week left and though I would like to continue, I may not be able to due to the workload I have for school. But a couple of hours may be something I can do (Joan, undergraduate student, freshman year).

These notes are a good example of field notes that are comparing what she was feeling before and what she is feeling afterwards. In these notes, Joan finds that as events are unfolding, she is finding some events that are contrary to her expectations. She comments that she had originally thought this work would be "putting up with nonsense" but that now it is a stress reliever. While she did not anticipate these visits to be as enjoyable, she now finds them to be relaxing. In the process of questioning her original ways of thinking which included anxiety about the project, she is now discussing the humor in the experiences and a sense of a "quiet satisfaction." Furthermore, she also appreciates the work of the full-time staff at the center and feels as though she might be able to contribute a few extra hours to the center, which is more than she had originally anticipated doing.

Joan also writes about some interesting changes in her thinking as she ponders the last day at the adult day care center:

Before: Tomorrow is my last day at the day care center. Surprisingly, I am quite sad about it. Usually I don't like to do volunteer work, but this was fun. And though the elderly people can be a handful, I had a good time and learned more from them about life than anyone else. They don't come out and say how we should appreciate being young or having our whole lives ahead of us, but it shows through their actions. Some just sit and wait to leave, others seem to be waiting to die because they have nothing left. Yet some are energetic and talkative. Those are the ones that I am determine (sic) to be like. Rhonda is definitely my favorite. Though she had a hard life from her childhood and even through her marriage, she still was so happy and made the best of any given situation. Today she is still very close with her children and grandchildren and seems to still love life. She makes the best of her time at the day care center, making friends, doing the various activities, and just talking about anything at all. So now that I've made friends at the adult day care center, I will miss them. I would love to go back and see them, and some of us have said we probably will before the end of the year, but I just don't have a lot of time. I am so busy with school and with everything else that it is hard for me to make time for volunteer work. However, I do enjoy it and hopefully will be able to do more in the future. I am no longer anxious or nervous to go to the center. I am comfortable with the elderly and the people that work there (Joan, undergraduate student, freshman year).

Joan explains in the above set of field notes how she is no longer anxious about going to the center, which is the opposite of her feelings before she started the project. She was very nervous at the beginning of the project, and by the end she did not have those feelings. In fact, she even mentions in the previous field notes that the visits are a stress reliever for her, and keep her mind off the daily stress of college life. Joan also writes that these experiences have shown her that the elderly at the center have a way of letting her know she is lucky to be young, and that she has her life before her. What is also interesting is that she has started to look at service-learning as a positive, and not a negative, experience. In this passage, she mentions that she enjoys the service-learning, to the point of wanting to do it again. Therefore, she believes she may include service in the future.

Joan also goes further into her thoughts and feelings in these notes by stating that she has learned about life at the center, and there are people there who she wishes to emulate. While she does mention that some of the elderly are pessimistic, she hopes to be like one of the positive clients, Rhonda, one day. She admires this woman at the center who is friendly and outgoing, and willing to try anything. Joan has actually found a role model for her future, as well as finding friends. By analyzing her field notes, we can see how Joan's attitude has evolved from dread to awe. These notes display some of the benefits students enjoy in the service-learning project. Although Joan does mention that the elderly are "a handful" she also notes that there are different types of people present, which is a good observation. While Joan begins to write generally about the elderly as a group, it is more descriptive notes that she takes when she discusses an individual. In this case it is Rhonda who she admires. A good note to add here is to try to focus in on a specific individual in order to provide the reader with detail, rather than generally, and also vaguely discussing a group. It is also interesting for the reader to note that despite Joan's original anxiety about the project, she was able to make friends and did see the elderly people as a good source of knowledge.

The second section of the paper in this Introduction to Sociology class required the students to reflect on their experiences. In this reflective portion the student may wish to discuss the prior thoughts and feelings s/he had and compare them to the actual events. Alternatively, the student can connect their reflections to some of the course readings. For example, in classes that required students to tutor children, I have suggested that they correlate their findings to readings on education or social stratification. In classes in which students participated at homeless shelters, where they have interacted with clients and site supervisors and served food, I have asked them to discuss their experiences and compare or contrast them to the course readings in homelessness or social stratification. At times, students might refer to readings on deviance, or social interaction, which is also acceptable, of course. When students in past classes have done intergenerational service-learning, or assisted the regular staff at an Adult Day Care Center or a nursing home, I have suggested that they use the readings in the aging section of the course to help with the writing process. The students can also discuss methodology when writing their papers, such as evaluating participant observation as a research technique, and weighing its advantages and disadvantages. The goal of this second section of the paper was a requirement for the project so that the service-learner would reflect on the experience, and to start making connections by incorporating course readings. The faculty advisor can provide you with additional course readings, which can enable you to connect the course with the service-learning in appropriate ways for the course. The goal of the next chapter is to examine reflection thoroughly including an analysis of why it is such an integral feature of service-learning.

# CHAPTER

# 7

# Writing Service-Learning Papers: What Is Reflection, Exactly?

Reflection can be vague and hard to understand because doing reflection requires involving yourself in the dual purposes of exploring yourself, in addition to the course topic. The reason reflection is integral to the service-learning project is precisely because it does include the researcher. Reflective writing allows the service-learning researcher to explore how the assignment has changed or altered his or her interpretations, perceptions, or lives in any way.

There are several topics you may consider reflecting on in regard to the service-learning visits. One issue the service-learners may choose to reflect on is the features of their everyday setting, in comparison and contrast to the setting at the service-learning site. For instance, consider your everyday environment and how it influences you, how you feel in it, and how comfortable you may or may not be in it.

Contemplate and write descriptively about your physical setting in your home or dorm room. Think of those "things" you may have available such as lamps, chairs, beds, rugs, television sets, computers, bathrooms, etc. Describe the sights, sounds, and scents that surround you in this typical setting. Then, consider those distinct features of your service-learning site. Write about the sights, sounds, and scents that are a part of the service-learning setting. When you write about these two different settings, it will be a good method to use in order to describe where you are, as well as how your own senses and your sense of self are affected in those two environments.

Another great reflective technique to follow is for you to consider how you think you are being viewed by clients and site supervisors, and to describe if you think the view that others have of you is accurate, ill-conceived, or flattering. You can think about those different views others may be having, and write up an evaluation of what those views may be, and how they make you feel. For example, if you perceive that the view they have of you is inaccurate, does that perception make you feel uncomfortable at the site or does it not affect you in any way, shape, or form?

The service-learner may also evaluate his/her view of what the clients and site supervisors are going to be like, and consider how that perception affects how the clients may be affected by the service-learning site visits. In other words, if the clients or site supervisors feel that they are being viewed in a negative way, this may make them uncomfortable around service-learners. In all this hurly-burly of activity what each person may be thinking of the other person, it can also be an intriguing topic to write about what happens when those different parties interact. For instance, is it a chaotic or calm interaction? Also, were you uniquely surprised by the calamity or the calmness of the intersection of service-learner, client, and site supervisor? You may choose to describe the comfort level, or the tension, or the camaraderie that happens for each and every visit. By comparison of the field notes of the different visits, you can consider whether your views of the people you are learning from are any different than before the site visits began. Alternatively, you can consider whether their views of you may have been changing over time. Of course, it is difficult to figure out at times what others are thinking, but the writing of your thinking in your notes can reveal certain areas of interest about what is going on at the site, and it can also develop into a very careful and descriptive accounting of what you may be experiencing on these visits.

You may consider describing your "metamorphosis" over the time period of the site visits. You may choose to describe the change you have experienced during the project, if you have altered your habits, or changed your thinking in some way, these are other provocative areas to write about in your paper. In this section, you may decide to document your interest, or lack of interest, in doing service-learning in the future, or you may indicate if your field of interest has changed. In other words, your interest in service-learning may be to continue your civic involvement through your college career. Or alternatively, your service-learning may have piqued your curiosity about other fields of interest such as learning more about political science, anthropology, sociology, biology, foreign languages, public administration, education, and so on.

It may also be enlightening as part of your reflective writing to discuss your motivations in getting involved in the service-learning project. Examine in written form why you were originally interested in participation. Your goals may have been to get extra credit, to impress the faculty advisor, to have a community involvement project on your resume, to help others, and to learn more about the subject area. Investigation of the motivations and goals you had at the inception of the project will be a good way to reflect on the meaning the project has for you. You may analyze your reasons for participating originally and find that, as you proceeded, your goals have changed. For instance, you may have started the project as an international student in the United States, hoping to find our more about American culture by going to an adult day care facility for people who need care on a daily basis, and not looking forward to the process of aging. You may then have ended the project looking forward to growing old, having good friends, and still enjoying good times. In some cases, what you originally intended may have happened, but, in addition, other transformative benefits have occurred. Writing about your service-learning project as an ongoing process over time can be enlightening and informative for yourself as well as to the reader.

If you have chosen to examine your motivations for the service-learning project you may also choose to describe why clients are at the service-learning site, or why site supervisors choose to work there, or why faculty advisors do get involved also. By determining the motivations of these various participants, you may discover it is intriguing to note how the different motivations intersect, and how your reasons for involvement may differ, or be similar to the goals others have for the project.

Further, you may consider the consequences of the service-learning for yourself, or how others describe what has been accomplished at the site. In this type of reflection, you may write on how you think others would evaluate what you have done at the site and what will come from it in the future. Try to contemplate what signs there have been of "service" according to yourself, your group, the clients, and the site supervisors. Would everyone involved see your involvement as "service," or as something else that could be described by using another term? The interesting comparisons here would be on your own ideas of consequences as contrasted to the others included in the project. If you consider goals and purposes and consequences differing among the different participants, how does that shed light on the "usefulness" of the project if at all? In this type of reflective exercise the service-learner can write about the convergence of different goals and/or the existence of one common theme amongst different people's interpretations of consequences.

Reflective writing can also be connected to the terminology used to describe the service-learning. Students can examine whether or not "service-learning" adequately describes the project, or if "charity" seems a more adequate term. The student can also consider the term "volunteer" and discern whether or not what s/he did could be best recognized as volunteerism. This exercise of examining the correct, or most appropriate terminology, can allow you to analyze what you did, evaluate the outcomes, and, also, can shed more light onto the current terms used in this area, and possibly, point to a more suitable vernacular.

The service-learner may also consider writing in his/her reflections about whether or not s/he feels there has been any value found in the service-learning project. Service-learners may choose to examine how, or if, individual prospects have changed as a result of the work, or if they feel there have been any results observed in what they have done at the service-learning site. Value can be discussed according to what has been gained in the project for the different people involved. You may choose to describe the value experienced by the clients, the site supervisors, the faculty advisors, or other service-learners. You can also reflect on your own personal gain in regard to the project, or you can describe how you think you have gained academically, professionally, personally, or monetarily on the basis of the service-learning site visits.

In this example, a student discusses what she has gained from the service-learning project in the Reflective section of the paper assigned in my Introduction to Sociology class:

> In conclusion, the elderly people at the Adult Day Care Center are more than just old people; they are exactly like me with just a few more wrinkles and experiences. I have learned more from them and this service-learning project than I ever could in a classroom. I think that they learned from me too. They were inquisitive about school and my family. By talking to young people, happy memories from their childhood and young adult lives were brought back. Although not all of the elderly people were pleasant, overall, I had a very good experience (Joan, undergraduate student, freshman year).

This is a good example of a description that displays some soul-searching which went on during the service-learning project. It does not seem that this writer took the experience lightly, but spent some time thinking about it, and examining the impact s/he had on the site clientele, as well as the influence they had on her. Contemplating this project led this student to point out the commonality of experience we all have, for instance, she did not find the people she visited to be very different from herself. In understanding the way that we all have similar existences, and the way we all face certain obstacles, this example indicates a change of attitude between thinking that the clients were different and believing they were just like her. The people who she visited were not "just old people" but were like her except for "a few more wrinkles and experiences."

By reaching this type of conclusion, Joan was trying to bridge the gap between "us" and "them," trying not to assume that other types of people were different from "us" and discovering in this process that there were unfair stereotypes at work against the elderly. Joan was able to discuss the reciprocity involved in the experience when she discusses how she learned from the elderly, and how they learned from her as well. She notes that it was not a one-sided relationship in which she only benefited from the experience in obtaining course credit and knowledge, but that also the site clientele were able to relive some youthful memories. Noting that the service-learning relationships were more than one-way exchanges, and were more similar to two-sided partnerships, indicates that Joan was able to discuss how both parties were positively influenced by this project, as well as being able to analyze the situations carefully and in full detail.

By clearly describing the site visits, and making a strong conclusion to the reflective portion, it seemed Joan was able to avoid the dehumanization that could occur when an individual believes a stereotype about another. The ability that Joan had to discuss the commonality of experiences, as well as the reciprocity involved in the exchanges, meant that Joan was involved in the project wholeheartedly, and prepared to write about it in absorbing detail.

It may be that the student chooses not to focus on what they have gained from his or her service-learning experiences. Service-learners may also choose to reflect on the *limits* of their work, or what the service-learners did *not* feel they were able to accomplish during the service-learning project. Some service-learners may find that when compared to the widespread nature of certain social problems such as elder neglect, poor educational systems, and homelessness, what they have done at the service-learning site is not making as much difference as they would have hoped.

This next example displays the reflective portion of the writing assignment which describes the differences or similarities between the thoughts and feelings one has before the site visit, and then compares and contrasts them to the sentiments one has after each visit. The service-learner is encouraged to outline his or her preconceptions about the upcoming event, and then compares them to actual events. This is helpful because the student gets the opportunity to disclose some ideas which s/he may not have been permitted to express in any other forum. Not only are these conceptions disclosed, but they are also held up to a scrutinizing light to be examined and analyzed. What is important for the reflective portion is the analytical work that is done and not the change in the ideas, or how the student's preconceptions were stereotypical. Therefore, the student may have his or her preconceptions substantiated, and not necessarily changed, and still could have done an excellent job at reflection as long as the notes are analyzed.

In this particular example, a student examines her preconceptions prior to the service-learning event and compares them to thoughts and feelings after the project:

> When I found out that our fourth credit site was going to be the Adult Day Care Center, a day care for the elderly, I expected to have the usual experience with the patients that I had had in the past. My usual experience was to have a constant feeling of guilt and sympathy for these people, not because they were old and sickly, but because they were forced to go

to a day care which was dirty, disgusting, and not fun, where they were treated poorly. Unfortunately, I have visited places with these horrible conditions and that is perhaps why I am so strongly against sending any of my family members to a place like it. But this place has dramatically changed my view and perception of elderly day care centers. Not only is the center extremely clean and well managed, the clients are catered to both mentally and physically. The clients are constantly on the go whether it be playing games, exercising, singing, or just relaxing, the whole day is structured around pleasing them and keeping them happy (Tracey, undergraduate student, freshman year).

Tracey decided to investigate the difference between their preconceptions and post-conceptions when analyzing her field notes for the reflective portion of the paper. By investigating these differences, Tracey is comparing the dread she had before the event, to the altered view she has after the service-learning project. By examining these feelings and thoughts about the assignment, Tracey has been able to express an appreciation for the day care center she visited for this service-learning project. While it seems that Tracey is relieved with the conditions at the adult day care center she visited, she notes how she was expecting to observe the deteriorated conditions she saw in past projects. This experience then has indicated for Tracey how one can discover the unanticipated consequences in different types of settings.

Tracey also decided to write on her motivations behind getting involved in the service-learning project, and this description revealed another kind of unanticipated consequence:

Also, I chose to do this project because I wanted to earn the fourth credit, but when I entered the Adult Day Care Center, my earning an extra credit had nothing to do with my being there. I was there for the clients, they were my priority and I did not want them to feel that they were second on my list. I never really thought they actually appreciated me. I just assumed that they never really considered that I was there for them, but rather just randomly happened to be there. It was not until my second visit when Laura said to me, 'you are such a doll, you really do not have to do this for me' when I was helping her on the swings. I told her that I wanted to help her and that it was my pleasure. She then said, 'I just want you to know I really do appreciate you staying with me.' I was so touched by this. It was as though she were reaching out to me. It was one of the few times where I actually saw Laura being serious and meaning what she said. I felt extremely honored that she had noticed that I was devoting time to her. I was happier to know that she was enjoying my company. It is times like this that make this type of work/service worth it. The fourth credit essentially means nothing. It carries no sentimental value whatsoever. The quality time with the clients is what enabled me to continue my service (Tracey, undergraduate student, freshman year).

In this set of reflections, Tracey is investigating the value of the project, what benefits the site visits had for her, and how she would describe the value of the work. In examining her motivations for being involved in the project, she noted that her original reason was no longer a priority when entering the site. At first, her motivation was to earn a fourth credit for the course. In this Introduction to Sociology course at Bentley College, if the student completed an extra 20 hours of service, s/he could receive a fourth credit. Each course usually had 3 credits, so that if a student participated in three fourth credit options, they could receive the equivalent credit found in one course.

In the passage above, Tracey defines how her original motivation for participating in the project, the fourth credit, becomes irrelevant and has "no sentimental value whatsoever."

In this very interesting passage, Tracey is exploring how a priority can become secondary based on some significant interaction. Therefore, what you can assume is your reason for doing service may not necessarily continue to be your primary motivation as the project continues. What was valuable to this student at the onset of the project lost its value after some interaction with a woman who was affected by Tracey's consideration. To explore your reasons and motivations for being involved at the onset of the project is an interesting way to reflect, because you can analyze the way those goals may be altered through the course of the service-learning project. In Tracey's case, a very practical motivation, course credit, was replaced by a caring and sharing impulse. It is insightful to examine the patterns of changes to motivations when doing service-learning, to see if there are any changes, and if those goals have a typical trajectory. For instance, you may chose to analyze if it seems that your motivations are altered by any one turning point, or if they differ according to interactions with different people.

Tracey also reported a change in how others perceived her presence affected the setting. She originally believed she was not being noticed for her work, or that the site clientele thought "she just randomly happened to be there." However, after she received a compliment, she realized that she was having an impact on the people at the site, that she was appreciated, and her work was being noticed. Realizing the positive effect she was having with Laura, allowed Tracey to recognize how the site clientele not only appreciated her, but were deeply affected by her presence. This realization of the results she had on others displayed for Tracey that she was making a difference.

## Further Suggestions on Reflection

The goal of this section on reflection was meant to offer you practical advice on how to reflect on your service-learning experiences, including detailed ways to write about your experiences. If you are still grappling with these concepts, and want additional ideas, you may consider comparing and contrasting different experiences that you have had in the past as a good way to encourage reflection. You may consider comparing this service-learning experience to other service-learning experiences you have had in the past, or you may discuss how this writing exercise differs from others you have experienced. If you wrote your reflections alone or in a group you can compare how this project differs from past writing experiences. Also, try to include how you would define past and present projects in terms of how much was learned. For example, discuss what you learned about service-learning writing as a collaborative project or as a solitary endeavor.

Whether your writing exercise was done alone or with others, you may consider that you have discovered a great deal more about yourself than you previously imagined and that this self-examination would make a good topic for your service-learning reflection. Think about your cultural assumptions, values, expectations, and how they impacted your experience with service-learning (Watters and Ford, 1995). You may also describe your service-learning team, and how they affected your learning experience, or if you worked on your own, you can write about what you learned about yourself involved in a solitary project.

Other issues to explore would be how the class itself taught you more about the social issue surrounding the project, and if the course helped you to understand the community-based organization, its clients, and the site supervisors. If there was an aspect that was not covered, which should have been covered in the course, you might consider writing about how to include another section to the class.

These topics will stimulate your analysis of the service-learning experience and help you to focus on the social issues. Approaching the writing by focusing on a social problem may challenge you to think of solutions to the problems, and to assess if, and how, the community-based organization meets the needs of the clients. You might also include the political ramifications in your writing, particularly in regard to how politics impacts the organization, including how political issues impact the survival or growth of the site in the future. By focusing on the future of the community-based organization, the student may also be asked to speculate on alternative arrangements s/he thinks may improve the organization. Again, you may discuss what you think will be your service-learning plans for the future and explain your reasons for planning that particular level of civic involvement in your future prospects.

## The Final Analysis: Making Connections

The third and final section of the paper I generally assign for the service-learning project is the formal section. The assignment calls for this part of the paper to be well-written and clear, and to systematically take examples from the field notes and analyze them according to course concepts, readings, class discussions, or lectures. This section needs to be written with a summary, conclusion, and well-formulated paragraphs. This is the section in which the student is encouraged to make the correlations between the course material and the service-learning experiences using organization and analysis. The students have the choice about whether they wish to focus on one theme for this section, or to discuss several themes in their writing. The third section can be thought of as the "top of the pyramid." The pyramid is symbolic of the final part being built upon the "building blocks" of field notes and reflections. If the field notes and reflections are weak, and not written correctly, the third section becomes difficult to write well. The field notes should be descriptive, detailed, and written directly after the site visits, and they can be the strong foundation they need to be for a comprehensive paper. Reflections are also essential, and the student should ask themselves provocative, in-depth questions, and do some soul-searching in order to do some good work in the second section.

The next example of a service-learning paper indicates a great deal of thought and insight that went into the service-learning project, and is from the final and formal section of the paper. As previously noted, this section requirement was for the student to apply course concepts, readings, class discussions or lectures to the experiences:

> A significant part of an elderly person's life is the criticism and insults that they must endure. They become victimized because of their physical ailments and mental status even if they aren't that decrepit. The stigma, or "permanent identity spoilage" is the cause of this victimization and criticism (Newman, 1998). For most of their lives, the elderly people were just like everyone else, active and socially acceptable. Now that they are in wheelchairs, cannot talk very well, or have Alzheimer's disease, society in general assumes that it is okay to discriminate against them because they are different. I found this evident in the way Mary, one of the workers there, treated Lois. When it was time to leave, Mary yelled at her and pulled her to the bus, treating her like a child. Just because Lois is old, doesn't mean that she is incapable of acting like a normal person by going to the bus by herself. I think it is unfair of Mary to assume that Lois couldn't do things alone.

Additionally, the most common type of criticism occurs just in passing. Each day people make fun of or gawk at elderly people just because they have some differences. The stigma of old age, wrinkles, limping, memory loss are all part of getting old, but they still cause others to talk about them. In turn, the elderly do not feel normal and feel victimized by fellow human beings. It may cause depression and other mental ailments if it occurs regularly which eventually causes more long term effects on the older person (Joan, undergraduate student, freshman year).

Joan used course concepts such as victimization and stigma to describe the treatment of the elderly in American society. Joan discussed in detail what she felt were the effects of victimization on the elderly individual, and the ways that others affected the elderly and can impact their self-identity. By examining how the stigmatized individual is affected by the treatment of others, Joan was able to "take the role of the other," or place herself in the position of the elderly person and imagine how the discrimination must feel. Joan discusses the change that can occur to a person over the long-term if she must experience this type of discrimination and criticism. By exploring these topics of stigma, discrimination, and victimization, Joan was able to identify and apply key course concepts effectively, indicating she had a good grasp of these ideas, and could also use them to describe service-learning experiences. The student also indicated the ability to use the methodology of participant observation to understand another's social world by putting herself into another's social situation, or "taking the role of the other."

This next example is taken from the third section of a student's paper who participated in a service-learning project with children at a homeless shelter:

Prior to working with the children I fell victim to a common norm of society. This misinterpretation was that often, deviant labels are more often applied to lower-class than middle-class adolescents. This article was written by William J. Chambliss in *Sociology: Exploring the Architecture in Everyday Lives*. The way that the roughnecks were viewed was similar to the way in which I viewed the children because I thought them to be poor. The Saints were always well dressed, and excellently behaved. As a result they were thought to be the good boys and were often shown mercy by the police. The Roughnecks were treated differently. Just because they were not so well dressed, or well mannered, they were seen as the bad boys in town. Even though they engaged in the same type of mischievous activities that the Saints did they were viewed as more of a menace to the public. I myself fell victim to this way of thinking. Just because I was going to the Salvation Army, a place that I associated with poverty, I thought the kids would not be well behaved. Usually poor children do not have as much supervision because of the fact that their parents have to leave them alone all day to make money or they just don't care. As a result children from these families in society are seen as too rambunctious or as hoodlums. I fell victim to the same way of thinking. Although to my fairness this way of thinking was held true by the first boy we worked with, who did not listen, painted on the floor, and squirted me with the juice box, it did not for many of the others I talked to. Especially Carl, the boy I felt I bonded with. As a result I have learned to treat all situations as they come and to use a more objective point of view (Paul, undergraduate student, freshman year).

Paul's writing for the third section of the paper is excellent in many ways. Firstly, he successfully includes himself in his work by incorporating his own feelings and preconceptions about the site visits. He indicates for the reader how he has some preconceived notions of the type of child he will discover at the site. These notions regarding the behavior of the children are described as his expectations even if they are stereotypical, and based on the social class of the child. He discusses how he thinks the parents may not care about disciplining the child, and expects the children to misbehave. By comparing his expectations to his actual experiences, he discovers the class bias in his assumptions, and admits he has fallen victim to those misconceptions. Paul displays his ability to question the original assumptions he had prior to the site visits.

Paul also shows how he has analyzed the course reading, and extended that analysis to compare one researcher's findings to his own discoveries on his site visits. By making connections to the course he has achieved one of the key objectives of service-learning: using course materials to analyze one's own experiences. By using the service to learn the course, Paul has accomplished two goals: applying course materials, and assisting community organizations. Further, he has described his preconceptions about the children he would assist, and in many ways has included himself as an active agent in the study. Paul includes a through analysis of his own thoughts and beliefs, and also discusses how the project has altered his perceptions and changed his habits. He mentions at the end of the excerpt how he has learned how to "take situations as they come," and will try to maintain an objective interpretation of the situations in which he finds himself.

Reflections, and doing final analyses, both offer you an opportunity to write about a topic and to include yourself simultaneously. When you include yourself you are adding a dynamic dimension to your writing, you will be able to include what you discovered about others as you examine more about yourself. This reflective technique and writing as a final analysis may be exciting, but it does bring your writing to an uncharted territory. As you try to maneuver around these uncharted areas, you may get lost or make mistakes, which is common in this type of navigational exercise. The next section offers some tips on how to avoid an obstacle course when doing this type of writing for a service-learning project.

# 8 Writing Service-Learning Papers: On Avoiding Some Common Mistakes

One common mistake when writing a service-learning paper is to add to stereotypes rather than taking them apart. If we blame the individual for his/her status in life, rather than focusing on social problems for causing difficulties in individual's lives, service-learners can be reinforcing stereotypes. One way that stereotypes can be reinforced is to arrive at negative conclusions about people with scant evidence. To see inequality as a result of negative character flaws would only serve to substantiate, rather than negate racist, ageist, or classism ideas about people. Here are two examples of students who have arrived at stereotypical conclusions:

> It is so funny how each one of the elders has a different style of dress. Some look preppy, while others seem not to care how they look. Some ladies carry their purses around the entire morning. They are always ready to go! However, most of them are just wearing a sweater and a pair of pants. They are so cute. These people are like little children.
>
> Life is a cycle…you start off as a child, go through the stages of adolescence, reach adulthood, and so on, until you become an elder. When people become elders, they get to a point where they start acting as children once again. They cannot go to the bathroom by themselves, they cannot eat by themselves, etc (Amy, undergraduate student).

> We were put in charge of games for them. We were playing golf, throwing beanbags into holes, throwing rings onto a stick. We organized the games so that every one of the patients had a chance to play. Everyone took turns, and they all behaved themselves very well. At first, I talked to them as I was talking to my friends, which is that I gave mutual respect to those clients. After these three days, I realized I should treat them more like dependent children because they really do act like children (Al, undergraduate student).

> The Clients were screaming, jumping, and talking like little children. I thought the client's actions were very adorable (Al, undergraduate student).

In these three passages the students describe the elderly at an adult day care center as dependent and childlike. The consequences of this type of description are that the elderly people at the site are understood as in their present situations, of needing extra assistance during the day, and being dependent, due to their own character deficiencies and personality flaws. It would be more instructive to see the elderly as dependent due to reasons they have no control over, to emphasize that they are living in this manner due to social conditions beyond their control. For instance, it is possible that due to their advancing age, these clients are made to feel like children in their daily interactions, and that they have learned to behave in this way in their rounds of daily activity. It is also possible that they have fewer and fewer responsibilities in their lives than they used to, and have not had the opportunities available to exercise independence. Another unfortunate possibility in the lives of elders is that they may be victimized in home or institutional settings. When mistreated in different ways, one person's coping mechanism can be to act in an uneasy and demure way. If a person is made to feel they have less and less control over their life circumstances, and s/he is made to feel helpless, it may be that dependence is the only possible role to play. The result of these actions is for an observer to comment on their dependence with demeaning comments about how "adorable" the clients are, rather than commenting on the difficult conditions they may live under.

The emphasis on these types of cases for the writer should be on what is happening in the client's world to affect them in a certain way, rather than how it is somehow natural for an elderly person to revert to childhood. There may also be medical reasons for the clients' behavior, such as forms of dementia, which are not indicated in these passages. The assumption is that the people will inevitably act more like children as they age. This stereotype should be avoided as not indicating how the elderly individual is hurt by the outside influences over his or her life. This common tendency to blame the individual for his/her actions, rather than examining outside influences which cause these problems has been referred to as "blaming the victim."

One way to help combat reverting to stereotypes in your writing is to seek frequent feedback. Try to challenge the stereotypes in regular meetings with other students and professors to examine your experiences and to discuss and evaluate your writing. Other participants can have unique perspectives that shed light on some of your interpretations of the site visits. It is also helpful to focus on individuals rather than on groups in your writing. When the service-learner writes about the group, the individual characteristics can get lost. Writing about "the clients" or the "elders" has a way of losing sight of specific individuals and what they are doing at the site. This next example avoids writing about the group as a whole and focuses in on one person, while avoiding victim-blaming. Eileen successfully described how this elderly woman was affected by the outside conditions in her life:

> The third time I went to the adult day care center I was glad to go back and see the people. I knew they were expecting us and that they were happy to see us. On the other hand I still felt awkward going there. I admit that it was not very pleasant for me being there.
>
> The program we had to do was the same as every other time. We either had to participate and help out in something collectively or work individually with one person. I took place [sic] in the group projects and helped a staff member to organize a game for them.
>
> As we were playing the game, a woman in a wheelchair insisted on going to the restroom. Everybody refused taking her and this matter shocked me. The manager was telling her that it was not her turn to go to the bathroom and that she should wait. Of course this lady got mad and started shouting at the manager. She was telling her that she really needed to go to the toilet and what mattered if it was not her turn since she had this necessity and had to use the bathroom?
>
> The manager did not change her opinion and did not pay any attention to what she was telling her. I felt so bad because the woman in the wheelchair was absolutely right. Why should they control her life? She had the need to go to the toilet; if she could walk she

would be able to go by herself, nobody would prevent her from going. Then why do they prevent her now?

And if that was not enough, she saw me and told me: 'Please young lady take me to the toilet, I really need to go.' I did not know what to do. My heart and logic were telling me to take her, but the staff was telling me not to pay attention to her and just leave her complaining. She was looking at me in a way that was really forcing me to take her. I felt like she was begging me. I believe it is very unfair not being able to go the bathroom because it is not your turn. This lady received this conduct because she was a minority; she could not use her feet. Seriously I was very upset and mad at the same time with the staff.

I tried not to listen to what everybody was saying because it made me feel even worse. Most of the other elder people there tell me: 'Why don't you take her? What's your problem? Come on, can't you see that she is suffering?' I did not know what to do. Especially, because all of them were against me as if it was my fault. It was a terrible feeling that occurred because I had to obey some rules, which were against my will (Eileen, undergraduate student).

Eileen's discussion is an interesting one because she is sympathizing with a client at the adult day care center and is also experiencing similar social control within the situation. While the client at the center is not allowed to be taken to the rest room, Eileen is also being told at the same time not to take her. Eileen identifies with the client's pain and position of helplessness because she wants to help, but is being told not to. At the same time, there are other clients who are urging Eileen to go against the wishes of the site supervisors at the center. If she takes the client to the rest room, Eileen would be directly disobeying the rules, if she helps the client, she would be doing what she wanted to do and would be listening to the other clients.

It seems that Eileen is being put in the unenviable position of being "in the middle" between the site supervisors and the clients in this conflict. It also seems that the clients are taking the position of the other client in opposition to the site supervisors. This conflictual situation would actually make for a good analysis because the service-learner can wonder how often these types of situations occur, or the service-learner can analyze how typical it is to have tension between clients and site supervisors. When there is some conflict between the clients and supervisors, it would be interesting to observe if the different groups demand different and opposing actions from the service-learner. If you are ever placed in this type of situation, it might help to get the advice of the other service-learners at the site, the faculty advisor, and the college placement coordinator, so that they can give you an objective opinion and tell you if this type of situation has arisen previously.

Eileen's description of the situation is an excellent example of how service-learners can relate to someone at the site who may be unlike them in some way, but still may feel they have to operate under the rules of the site supervisors. In this case, Eileen has not blamed the victim for the situation she has found herself in, but instead sees that there are rules to the situation that they both have to conform to against their will. Eileen has learned from the client the vulnerability of not having the ability to walk, and be dependent, rather than describing the client as losing her independence as part of returning to a childish stage of life.

Sam's experiences differed from Eileen's because he was able to identify with the clients in a way that he did not originally anticipate:

> Looking back, I found myself to be more open than I thought I would be with the clientele than I am with some of my friends at school. I was discussing certain things like marriage and relationships very openly. I think that I felt comfortable with those people because their opinions were unbiased, and because of the answers they gave me. Maybe I felt comfortable because I needed an answer from a person who had lived his life and had a lot to talk about, and I might not have felt comfortable talking about this with my grandfather (Sam, undergraduate student).

Sam's experiences indicate that he was able to disclose personal stories with the clients he met up with in unexpected ways and, he felt that they offered him an audience who was objective and experienced. In this way, he was gaining advice in previously unimagined ways with experienced people he probably would not have met in his daily life. This again is a positive way to relate to people who may be in a different life stage, but still have much to offer in the way of advice, and sometimes to be able to listen in an unbiased manner. This student was able to learn from the elderly, a population that he originally thought he would be servicing unilaterally but they also comforted him in a way that displays the powerful reciprocal influence of service-learning. Sam was also examining the way he was when he was with the site clients and found himself able to be more open than with his schoolfriends. He spoke freely because he felt he was speaking with people who were unbiased and wise.

In addition to being comforted by the elderly clients of the adult day care center, Sam also learned some powerful life lessons on his service-learning project.

> The adult day care center has changed my view about aging. Before going to the adult day care center I used to think that being old meant being miserable and handicapped. I used to fear getting old because I was afraid that when I became old I would start getting sick and death would come slowly upon me. I believed this after seeing my grandfather, grandmother, my mother's uncle, and my nanny die slowly…This resulted in them slowly losing sight, the ability to walk, and finally depression. I used to wish that I would die at sixty so that I would not have to go through those ugly stages of living. This all changed after going to the adult day care center. There I saw that not all old people have to go through those ugly stages and slow deaths. Some were, but a lot were fine. They participated in games, such as golf or darts. They talked and laughed. Now I believe that if I take good care of myself I would be able to better my chances to be like them. Also, I learned that I should appreciate life and what I have, and not take everything for as granted, [sic] because some people do not have those things (Sam, undergraduate student).

Sam describes, in the passage above, how some of his perspectives on aging have changed due to his visits to the adult day care center. He was able to identify with the elderly at the site, even though he was of a different age group, and imagine himself in their positions. For the first time, he wants to live a longer life because he saw how it was still possible to enjoy yourself in your later years. The service-learning allowed him to broaden his world view because he was able to see how those people in his life who died difficult and slow deaths might not be typical. Before the service-learning, his own perspective was not giving him the whole picture. Because he was familiar with a few people who died in tragic ways, he thought it would be true for everyone and that it would definitely be true for him. The important lesson for him to learn was that it was possible to live beyond sixty and to enjoy his later years.

By seeing himself in others, Sam was able to thrust himself into the future and to envision a different scenario for his later life. In this way, he was also able to have a more open mind about what life can be like as one ages. What he previously believed to be the "ugly" stages of living could be filled with laughter and talking, playing games, and being happy. Another important lesson that Sam was learning when he completed his service-learning project, was that he should not take the things he had in life for granted, and he should appreciate his youth because youth is fleeting. Sam was pleased and surprised that he was serving others and, at the same time, learning powerful life lessons.

Another reaction that the service-learner can have is outrage at the physical or social conditions they observe when involved in service-learning projects. This can lead to what has been referred to as "the white knight syndrome," which is when students position themselves as saviors, and feel they can work to alleviate the injustices of the beleaguered population (Hondagnueu-Sotelo and Raskoff). This "white knight syndrome" can negatively affect the student's grade when writing a paper on the service-learning project because it indicates a sense of superiority. The implication of white knight syndrome is that the service-learner is more capable of "saving" the clients than the clients are themselves. This can have the unintentional but damaging consequence of treating the client as an inferior, and can also reaffirm the stereotype of the homeless or elderly, for example, as being weak and ineffectual. The focus of the powerful "saving" the powerless only adds to the presumptions made about the site's clients as being helpless victims in need of rescue. Certainly, the clients may be very much in need of assistance, but their plight is usually much more accurately diagnosed by large social problems which one student cannot always remedy with a "quick fix."

Students in my classes have described this "white knight syndrome," and in these following passages you can see examples of it:

> On my way back I started comparing the thoughts I had before coming and my present thoughts. There was a wide contrast in the two of them. I had a feeling that I need to be here for some time. I felt sympathetic for these guys. I wasn't sure what was going on in their family but I knew that they weren't feeling good about their age. They were just strong and would not give up on their life. There was another lady without her teeth. She couldn't speak properly but she always wanted to express herself. This is the case of the people there. They wanted to be talked about or talked to. So I decided that now I need to change my opinion of the old and dying. I wanted to see them happy at least when I was there (Allen, undergraduate student).

> While driving to the adult day care center I felt good. I wanted to go there and listen to her again. I wanted to make her feel better. I wanted to see her smile and have fun. I wanted to make her dance (Allen, undergraduate student).

In these passages Allen remarks on the difficulties of the elderly people, and some of the obstacles they face. In this way, he really depicts an understanding for what the clients face every day, and how they have to remain strong in spite of severe life circumstances. Allen seems to be able to have a more open mind in that he discusses a change in his previous ideas about the people he meets and as he describes an increased sympathy. However, the understanding and sympathy that he expresses seems to be only a superficial empathy when he mentions wanting them to have fun, be happy, and dance. These notes indicate that Allen feels he can make people at the site happy. The writing reaffirms the stereotype of elderly people as weak and miserable, as well as indicating that the student may feel he is superior, due to his ability to make the people at the adult day care center feel contentment.

Allen's discussion of his service-learning project did indicate an increasingly open mind and a true identification with the elderly people at the site, but as indicated, there are parts that resemble the "white knight syndrome." The writing in the paper could have been corrected easily with more discussion in groups on how to challenge your own stereotypes when involved in these projects. It is of course helpful to get feedback on your work from other students and professors, and also to examine your role in the community. Try to examine with others, including the faculty advisor, what you will be able to do on the project, how you will be able to help others, either directly or indirectly. At times, site personnel are familiar with the clientele and know what goals are possible and probable. This might actually help to relieve a great deal of stress from your shoulders when you realize you will not have to put an end to world hunger, or prevent the injustices of the society, but that you can realistically expect to accomplish more tangible and immediate goals. Those goals may be feeding someone who is hungry, entertaining someone who is bored, or helping out employees that are overworked. Goals that are more "doable" may help you to more directly experience some rewards in your service-learning project.

One other possible mistake which is commonly made in service-learning papers has been referred to as "lecture regurgitation" (Hondagnueu-Sotelo and Raskoff). Lecture regurgitation is writing down information or concepts directly from lectures, without applying them to the case at hand. If you are writing down something that is from the lecture, text, or class discussions, you need to connect it to the example you are discussing. In this way, the reader can evaluate how the student has been able to analyze important course materials and is adept at applying them to various situations. The written application of course concepts or theories proves the student has understood the material. If the course lecture is written about, without connection to the service-learning experience, it does not indicate how the concepts or theories explain or clarify the service-learning situation. Professors are looking for the application of course materials in order to test the student's ability to make sense of the material with everyday life examples.

In this next example, Eileen rewrites lecture notes without connecting them to the example. She is reintroducing the situation of the woman who needed to go to the rest room at the adult day care facility. The italicized section is directly from class lecture:

> I saw some old people who, because of their age, could no longer walk and had to use wheelchairs. These people surely have lost their identity. They have come totally different from their past selves. It is very clear that these people are stigmatized. What especially helped me to come to this conclusion is the incident when a woman in the adult day care center, who was using a wheelchair in order to move, needed help to use the bathroom and nobody accepted to take her.
>
> She was told that it was not her turn to go to the toilet and they refused to take her so she got really mad. She betrayed herself with her attitude because by the things she said she showed that she felt like a minority and that she was inferior to others and stigmatized.
>
> *People who are stigmatized question their 'place' in social community and identity. Furthermore, some changes appear to others' perceptions about them, something that occurs [sic] changes in interaction. Those who lose their significant symbols have the lack*

*of opportunity to participate in situations they used to, they have fewer opportunities to interact because unfortunately people see them differently and finally they are deprived of approval.*

As a result these people interpret changes and become damaged personalities. It is very hard for them to adjust to their new self and accept their differences. They believe that they are 'outsiders' and that they cannot identify with the rest of the people, so they back off and keep as their own company their own selves (Eileen, undergraduate student).

Eileen is making points about the woman who was not assisted at the adult day care center that she identified earlier in her paper. Using this example, she is attempting to analyze the effect this situation had on the woman by using course concepts. The strategy itself is a good one, and is part of the directions to complete the journal paper. The student is required to use specific examples from the service-learning project and analyze them using course concepts, theories, readings, discussions, or lectures. Eileen only partially fulfills the requirements of the paper in the above example. She refers to an example and repeats part of the lectures that may explain the situation, but she did not indicate to the reader how stigma explains the woman's experience.

In the preceding example, the student writer has made some points about the situation which are not substantiated. In other words, she writes that the people "had to use wheelchairs" and have "surely lost their identity," but it is not clear why a wheelchair indicates lost identity. Certainly, there are many cases of people who use wheelchairs and have not lost identity. In this way, the observation seems to be unsubstantiated. The writer goes further to say that it was "very clear that these people are stigmatized," but it is not clear to the reader how they are stigmatized. A clearer description of what is meant by how they might be stigmatized would clarify and strengthen this point.

Further points about the writing example follow this discussion of a lack of connection and observations that are not explained. The writer claims the woman "showed that she felt like a minority," but it does not detail how the woman displayed that she felt that way, or if the woman had actually said that she felt like a minority. There is also a passage which states that the woman had "fewer opportunities to interact," which again may be true, but is not clear to the reader. The passage continues with a discussion of how the people feel as though they have "damaged personalities," and "cannot identify" with others; but it is not made apparent why, or how the people displayed these emotions. The elderly are referred to as feeling like "outsiders" but it is not clear how that type of generalization can be made.

The student's writing does bring up some interesting points about what this woman is going through, and how this situation may reveal something to us about how social structure affects lives. Perhaps certain elderly people do experience a feeling of being outsiders, but the reader does not know how this feeling has been expressed to the service-learner. In this case, it would have been helpful for the student to be involved in sharing her journal with other students or instructors, so they could provide feedback on the writing. Discussion of the topic with others involved in the service-learning project could have strengthened this paper substantially.

Other advice to service-learners in regard to analyzing the passage by Eileen is to avoid the common mistake that arises frequently, describing groups rather than individuals when discussing the people at the site. For example, when Eileen states "these people have lost their identity" it is not really clear how they lost it, or who is involved, or the exact ways this loss was incurred. It would be an improvement to write "this woman said she lost her identity when she lost her ability to conduct herself in the way she wanted to." Dealing with one person is more descriptive, detailed, and is easier to make the connection between what is going on, and how that translates to a loss of identity.

Also, when Eileen states "she betrayed herself with her attitude because by the things she said she showed she felt like a minority and that she was inferior to others and stigmatized," it is not clear what the woman said to display these emotions. If the woman said something which indicated an inferiority and a feeling of stigma it could have been included in the description to add to the analysis. This is how field notes are helpful, because what the woman said could be written down, and then quoted in the service-learning paper.

Another good addition to the paper is to include yourself in your writing in the form of a final analysis, just as much as you would in your reflection. In this final analysis the service-learner can include herself or himself as an active participant in the setting. Try to include yourself, and put yourself in another person's role in order to make sense of what is happening to him or her. For example, the service-learner can write "if I were her, I could see my identity change because I was denied bathroom access," "I could sense that I would be stigmatized if I could not walk myself," or "I would feel like I was an outsider if I was in this predicament." Including yourself in this type of writing adds strength to the description because you will be adding more depth to the description, and you are taking on the role of the other, which is an excellent methodology to use to gain insight into the world of others, and to come closer to understanding what others experience throughout the life course.

# CHAPTER

# 9    Working in Groups

Working in groups can be challenging but it can also be one of the most rewarding experiences to have when engaged in service-learning. You can meet people who have similar ideas and values and you can form bonds with one another. You can also meet people who have conflictual ideas, values, learn from them and form lifelong partnerships with them. There are certain steps to take that can help you when getting to know others, have them trust you and, if you are in a leadership role, to also have them complete tasks, which are necessary for a successful project.

The first step after you find out who the group members are is to get their names, telephone numbers, and e-mail addresses promptly. The next step you should take is to share your schedules, write down the times and days of your project, and begin to figure out when and where you should meet to get to the site on time. Try to also determine how you will get to the site, whether it is by car, walking, or public transportation. This will allow for some basic coordination so you will not have to scramble to get this information together later.

The next step is to make sure your group is communicating well about what are the goals and values of the project. After you are in agreement about those goals, you can accept them as a team and move on to an action plan. When possible, members should be aware of what their assignments will be and how their follow-through will affect the work of the whole group. This will make the members aware of how their lack of follow-through will not only affect their own work but may seriously impair the ability of the entire team to complete the project successfully.

Try to be as flexible as possible, it may be that a certain member might ask for your assistance, and though this may be a burden on you it is the nature of teamwork to be able to accommodate one another. If you are helpful to one another it will assist you in creating close bonds. Two of the basic ingredients to be found in a productive team environment is support and trust in one another, and if you help each other out, you will have done a lot to achieve the dual goals of trust and support. The best type of team scenario involves making decisions as part of a group forum, and if all the members of the team cannot meet, then informing the others when there has been a decision made in their absence. Also, always keep the lines of communication open so that all group members are aware and share the facts that are important to the group. If the group makes a decision, assure that the decisions will be made with the spirit of commitment by asking if anyone questions the decision and why they do.

It is possible that there may be some form of conflict in the group. If differences occur they should be dealt with, mediated, and handled. If necessary, discuss the problems with the team members, it is possible that these problems may be temporary, in that case the other team members might need to assume more responsibilities during the time it takes for the problems to be sorted out. If there is a group leader s/he should delegate responsibilities to other team members, in order to help out the individual who is having difficulties. If the problems the group member is experiencing are permanent, s/he might have to be asked to leave the group or s/he may have to resign. If there is not a team leader, then the group needs to agree as a whole who should do what until the absent team member rejoins the group.

The team members do not have to be close friends, and they might not necessarily become friends, what is important is that they trust one another, and understand what is expected of them for the project to be successfully completed. To have a good team means that your group collaborated, has been dependable, displayed perseverance, did negotiate, compromised, and were civil to one another. The very best of teams involve people who were able to motivate each other, and learned from one another (Dyer, 1995).

# Defining Diversity: Improving Intercultural Communication

This section is devoted to dealing with defining diversity, with discussing how to best deal with work teams that are diverse, as well as site supervisors and clients at community-based organizations who are from diverse cultures. There are many benefits to examining diversity when engaged in service-learning, including the advantage of being prepared. As a service-learner who is new to the community-based organization, you may wish to seek out more information on the culture of the agency. By the culture of the agency I am referring to what is common to discuss, what are topics to avoid, what are the dress codes; it is possible that these are issues which may also be raised if the agency has a formal training code. The site may include people of various ages, ethnicities, languages, races, and people with disabilities, and the service-learner may also be working on a team that includes students from different backgrounds. By learning more about dealing with intercultural communication, you will be able to change personally, and become knowledgeable in dealing with complex issues. By dealing with the different intercultural issues that arise, you will be more efficient at adapting, and you will be able to assume the role of others, or to walk in another person's shoes. When you do assume the role of others, or learn what another person's life is like, you can actually learn new perspectives, and judge situations in different ways. For example, if you were to meet a person who does not offer to shake your hand, you may initially be feeling confused or rejected. Later, through a broader perspective, you may find out that the person is not allowed to touch others due to his or her traditional cultural beliefs. In fact, not shaking your hand might have meant showing a sign of respect. For example, younger females may not shake an elder Cambodian man's hand because it can be interpreted as disrespectful. This new information about an act that originally was hurtful to you now has broadened your insight and understanding of the meanings others may have in their lives, and the way they interpret certain actions.

Now that we have investigated more about why it is important to explore the issue of diversity, let us take a more in-depth look at what we mean by "diversity." Specifically defined, you can refer to diversity as individuals with different races and genders. More broadly defined, diversity refers to persons with disabilities, personalities, linguistic, ethnic, racial groups, and ages. For the purposes of service-learning, and being involved in the interaction at the community-based organization, the broad definition of diversity will be used in this section.

The topic of diversity is also integral because a person's cultural background can affect the way the individual was socialized. An individual's cultural pattern includes his/her values, their communication and language use, rituals, situational behavior, roles, social status, time and space issues, and his/her relationship to the group (Cushner, 1996). These are learned through a socialization process that affects what a person is taught, and what s/he perceives is right or wrong. Learning values, and accepting them within a group, helps the members to achieve solidarity through agreement on a set of cultural norms. If a group shares similar values, the process of sharing assists them in getting along with each other, and achieving goals collectively. Values also indicate what an individual will find important, or what s/he would anticipate as useful. For example, assistive technology is valued in an individualistic culture in which self-sufficiency is valued. However, it may not be valued in a collectivistic culture in which a person is helped by others.

These cultural patterns are helpful to know more about so that the service-learner will understand that actions can be interpreted in a variety of different ways. Some groups also have rituals, such as lighting candles for the departed, which others may regard as ridiculous. Some groups have particular rules about how to behave in certain situations, and these rules will affect how you and they make sense of or evaluate what is happening. This may mean that the person's cultural training taught his or her to be quiet in a situation, or others may believe that you should be actively involved and participate vocally at all times. It is clear how you view the rules of the situation will also affect the way you interpret what happens there and also how to evaluate people. If you are socialized to be actively engaged in conversations, and you are in a place where people are always quiet, you may have to pay attention to what the rules are in particular places, and not be quick to judge those who have different communication styles at service-learning sites.

Different cultural groups have various ways of making sense about individual roles also, some may feel that fathers should be actively engaged in their roles as fathers, and some may feel that fathers should be willing to take a less-than-active role in parenting than the mother of the family. This difference in the belief about familiar roles are affected by culture and may influence the way the service-learner looks at and interprets the actions of the site clients or site supervisors. For example, if the service-learner discusses family roles with a site client and learns that the father takes a more passive role in parenting than the child's mother, that does not necessarily mean that the father does not take his role seriously as a parent, but means that his culture has a different standard and set of rules for participating in the parenting role. In some cultures, fathers only make major family decisions while mothers make choices related to day-to-day events of the children.

There may also be a certain status for a particular person in a role that differs from what the service-learner thinks is the "proper" status. For example, a father may not have much power in regard to the house, including meals and events, but may have a great deal of status in the family. Also, a mother may have control over what happens with the family, and in the house, but may be treated as an inferior outside the house. If a person from the outside is evaluating the mother's role outside the home, the outsider may not have the total perspective as far as what is the definite status of the mother. Thus, it would be important to have the father participate in meetings as well as the mother.

There are also other features of a person's cultural pattern that will have an impact on what the service-learner is interpreting at the site. For example, different people have different perspectives on time and space. Consider the individual who arrives late for an appointment. This person might be considered rude by other's who value punctuality. However, the late individual did not want to abruptly end a previous appointment because that action would have been interpreted as rude. Individuals participating in the second meeting are expected to know and understand this belief. Needless to say, this can create some difficulty when it comes to scheduling events, and predicting when participants will arrive and depart. Some feel violated if a person touches others while speaking. In some cultures, touching denotes hospitality. Some groups believe, after just one interaction, individuals can greet each other by hugging.

Further, there may be misunderstandings surrounding the individual's relationship to the group, or whether or not s/he is primarily interested in the goals of the group, or if s/he is primarily involved in "doing their own thing." Again, this may cause some miscommunication because the service-learner may not be aware of how to interpret others' actions, or how they are interpreting yours. This is why the best strategy is to learn what you can about cultural patterns, and how they affect a person's interactions, before you begin to come to conclusions about what those actions mean, and what they signify.

There are also other important factors involved when making sense of the context of a situation, and interpreting others' actions, which has to do with the way the service-learner feels at the site. One such feeling is belongingness which is a key concept in understanding diversity because people find it important to find their place within a community, and be a part of a group that we can identify with and enjoy shared interests with (Cushner, 1994). Because people find some status in groups, they can also feel a lack of identity when excluded from those social worlds, which brings about feelings of isolation and loneliness. One explanation for this need for belongingness is that some people find security in a group, and bonds have been forged prior to our entrance. Therefore, newcomers can enter a social situation, such as a service-learning site, without membership status in that group. This may increase the newcomer's sense of vulnerability and diminish his or her ability to add to a team effort because the service-learner does not know the rules of the situation and may feel alienated if s/he is rejected. One helpful recommendation is to just be aware that with time you will feel more of a sense of belonging, as you learn the rules of the situation, also, a sense of trust will be developed between the service-learner and the others. What I have done in this situation is make a prior "informal, get to know you" visit with someone who is credible in the agency. That way, I feel more accepted and others are more welcoming because I have developed a relationship already. Instead of an individual (either a service-learner, client or a site supervisor) feeling isolated, negative, and possibly even hostile, it is important to remember that there is a way to continuously negotiate communication between people, and in this way, decreasing feelings of being an outsider in an insider's world. Also, another important recommendation is to remember that an outsider may not be readily welcomed simply on the basis of being a newcomer to the scene, which has little to do with personal characteristics about the individual. Therefore, the reasons to reject or isolate the service-learner are not personal and should not be interpreted as a true reflection of the individual. Some community-based organizations may not positively react to an outsider's recommendations describing what's best for their communities. Thus, it is important to first develop a relationship that will result in a more trusting acceptance of each other's differences. This process of relationship-building can take time and should not be rushed. This is sometimes difficult for those who are outcome-oriented and want to get right down to business.

In addition to a lack of belongingness, another barrier which you may face initially during an intercultural experience while service-learning is anxiety. Anxiety at the beginning of such assignments should be understood as common and natural, and yet another topic to write about in your reflective notes on the project. You may be feeling uneasy, but you will be in situations that encourage you to grow as a person as you learn about different people, their values, and ways of life. As you learn more about diverse groups, it is likely that your experience will help to decrease the anxiety over the progress of the project. You may think that the anxiety you feel will make you more prone to common mistakes, but you will soon learn ways to avoid feeling anxious by feeling prepared.

The remedy for anxiety is to stay focused on your project and not to give up, especially if you think it is a worthwhile assignment that suits your educational and personal needs. If the service-learner does feel anxiety, it is common part of the process because new environments can cause that type of feeling but it is also common to be uncomfortable with the anxiety you experience, and to start to avoid the situation entirely. If you avoid the service-learning that is making you anxious, you may also come up with what may seem to be logical reasons for quitting the project. The best advice is again to not give up but to continue past this anxious phase, at a later date you will likely be feeling more comfortable with the guidelines of the project.

Those who do well in diverse settings are those people who can adjust themselves to the anxiety they may experience and adapt to fit into different situations that are going through a rapid ongoing process of change. For example if people are not responding to your own set of directions, or what is expected in different situations according to your cultural understanding of what is occurring, it may be because they are misunderstanding the information you are conveying. The service-learner who does well in this type of situation is one who can understand when there is a miscommunication, to ask questions and discover what is going on, and then they can behave according to the forthcoming answers. A changeable and flexible person, who can think on his or her feet is one who does well in this type of situation because s/he can change according to different rules that may be at work. The advantage to service-learning is that you can learn how to be a more adaptable and "think on your feet" type of individual with this type of experience in your background.

While the service-learners are examining their own interpretations of people's actions, including their own, they will also be in the position to analyze and learn more about themselves. In the process of self-exploration service-learners will be studying their own beliefs about others and may have to acknowledge they were wrong, or that they made a mistake. For example, some individuals in other cultures may appear to agree with what's being discussed when they really may not understand or disagree with information. Lack of follow-through at a later date may be interpreted as noncompliance. However, some individuals would not disagree actively in a group to avoid conflict or to save face of another individual. If they defined a situation in a particular way, and they described people in a certain way, and then discovered they were misinformed, they will also feel ashamed. People have different ways of dealing with the shame they may feel over a certain misinterpretation, some may acknowledge that they were wrong, and others may still continue to accept the prejudice because it is difficult to change one's beliefs. For the service-learning assignment, self-awareness can be facilitated by using reflective notes, or a writing project on your work. If you are alone with your thoughts, and know that no one will read these notes, you can feel free to write about how you felt in regard to a certain situation that upset the way you would normally look at common occurrences. You can come to a realization while writing that you may have been wrong, and that you may be willing to change your mind, but that although change is possible, the process of change, and adjusting to new information, can be a slow and difficult process.

Negotiating and learning through communication are excellent techniques to use in order to avoid having cross-cultural conflict. Another is a self-evaluation of one's values, beliefs, and communication style. If you know yourself, including becoming familiar with what is important to you, and learning about your communication style, you will be simultaneously discovering that you are expecting others to behave the way you do, and to think the way you do. If you are using your own communication style as a prototype, you are comparing others to yourself, including those elements of life you value; such as having an open mind about others, and the ways you expect them to live their lives. Understanding that others are permitted to live life according to their own rules, rather than the rules of others, will go a long way to helping people with different backgrounds get along peacefully.

After you have done some self-assessment, you may find that you do have some preconceptions and stereotypes about other groups or ethnicities. If that is the case, you may discover that those preconceptions are interfering with your ability to be objective in your dealings with the other person. You may find that you do not trust the person, which is a key element in any relationship. Or you may find that you are not giving the other person a fair deal, and instead you are only accepting the parts of the other person that substantiate your stereotypes. For example, we may tend to distrust people who do not maintain eye contact when conversing. However, lack of eye contact denotes respect for a person who is admired.

Communication is a key issue when dealing with diverse groups of people because they are frequently marked by some significant problems in communication. Whether the diversity is related to genders, ethnicity, age, or individuals with disabilities, groups can have different standards when it comes to verbal and non-verbal interaction. If it is difficult for trust and mutual understanding to form, due to the different styles in communication, and it may then take more time for bonds to grow between people. Because miscommunication can make one assume false motivations and intentions of others, the more prepared a service-learner is to accept different communication styles, and learn about them, the easier it will be to work together.

Nonverbal communication can differ depending upon the culture being either individualist or collectivist. At times, it is not always words that people communicate with, but we can also use nonverbal cues such as gestures, body language, and eye contact. The emphasis people place on nonverbal cues can be linked to the different types of cultures. Nonverbal communication is essential to be aware of, because people may rely on it in the absence of verbal cues. Further, nonverbal communication can carry powerful messages (Singelis, 1994). For example, if individuals from a collectivist culture were working together as a part of a team, but were having difficulties achieving a goal, they might not find it comfortable to complain to the site supervisor due to their interest in group harmony.

This emphasis on nonverbal communication to express feelings and interests has implications for service-learning. It may be instructive to pay attention to other service-learners, clients, and site supervisors members when involved in the service-learning project. Try to be sensitive to their cues, not only words spoken but also facial expressions, gestures, and postures that may indicate their feelings and intentions.

There are also some techniques to use to improve nonverbal communications between people, in order to help us understand and cope with differences. Firstly, be aware of what may be triggering certain emotions relating to how a person is acting, or what they are doing, and seek out explanations as to why a person may connect certain emotions to a particular activity. It may be standing too close in proximity according to one's particular taste, or making excessive eye contact, it is possible that their irritation is related to the way the person was socialized. If you are aware of the action, and paying attention to the way it affects others, you can have a better chance of stopping an unwanted emotion, such as anger, take over the situation. If you have an immediate negative reaction to a person on your team, then you may send out unintended nonverbal cues. These different forms of nonverbal communication, which could be interpreted in the wrong ways, can lead to giving others unjust labels. For example, we cannot assume that because someone has significant physical disabilities that this individual also has cognitive disability and cannot process complicated and detailed information. Instead of labeling someone, assume that you do not know everything you may need to know about these situations, and when you can, or when the situation is calmer, you can reinterpret what happened.

Also, be aware of your *own* nonverbal cues. If you are involved in a situation in which it seems like your own habits are offensive to the other individuals present, try to alter your habit in order to keep the group in harmony. This is difficult because we are not generally used to monitoring ourselves to fit any situation, but it is possible that when you pay attention, you may notice you are doing something that is causing a distance to form between you and others. If you are able to match your behavior to suit the communication style of others, it can go a long way toward promoting successful teamwork and can foster long-term friendships (Singelis, 1994).

It may help to not assume you are going to be at odds with a person simply because they are from another country, or have another skin color, but to try to use negotiation if you do run into difficulties. Negotiation refers to working on the meanings in different cultures by a particular gesture, comment, or behavior. This type of negotiation is more of an informal and open exchange of information, or pathway of communication, so that diverse people understand how they are being interpreted by others. If an informal negotiation is uncomfortable, and there are objective people available who would discuss more formally the significant symbols of different cultures, then the service-learner may choose that type of service offered by faculty advisors or site supervisors.

Strategies used in negotiation can also lead to transforming the *differences* found in diversity into *advantages* (Northcraft, et al., in press). By discovering more about each other's culture, it is possible to learn, and expand on, and extend your capabilities. For example, if individuals from a collectivist culture discuss their patterns of interaction with people from an individualistic culture, they may discover that each type of society has successful techniques that are productive. Service-learners, clients, and site supervisors may also learn through negotiating that members of the groups do find the benefits of the different approaches appealing. They may also begin to utilize these techniques when doing their own problem solving. Negotiating differences can be advantageous when learning new ways to solve difficult problems, and when learning the strategies of coping in various circumstances.

Preparation includes knowledge of how to deal effectively with people from cultures that are different from your own. It is helpful to learn one aspect of a culture that may differ, that is being either of the individualist or the collectivist type. An individualistic culture primarily relies on the rights of the individual being upheld above all else, the collectivist culture puts its emphasis on group harmony. This type of culture that the individual is socialized in can influence his/her work habits. For example, American culture focuses on individualism, and "doing your own thing" is important, and Americans are more likely to focus on what *you* want to do and how *you* want to get your goals accomplished. In a culture based on collectivism, the group's needs are paramount, rather than the individual's. Activities that are best suited to those in a collectivist society are those that adequately meet the needs of the group. Subsequently, when there is conflict in a collectivist culture, the good of the group is most highly valued, in an individualistic culture, the individual's needs are of the utmost importance. These two different types of cultures can cause some difficulty in terms of understanding what type of behavior is suitable, especially if it varies from what is typically acceptable behavior. For example, the person from an individualist type of culture may do what s/he can to call attention to himself or herself, in order to receive praise and recognition on the completion of a project. This type of behavior may not be acceptable to the person who is from a collectivist type of culture, because it may be looked upon as the individual calling too much attention to themselves and his/her own work, which takes the limelight away from the group.

It is helpful to remember that dealing with people from different social worlds does not necessarily have to create conflict. The problem is when people categorize each other into specific groups, one group can be treated as outsiders and the others as insiders. This is commonly referred to as the "out-group" or the "in-group." If different members of the group are categorized, and then treated differently, or discriminated against, then the team may be impeded from functioning at an optimal level. This is true not only of site clients, but also the service-learners themselves, when discriminated against inequalities of power and influence are reinforced. You may discover through service-learning that the people that you meet at the site are also differentiated into in-groups and out-groups. For instance, the site supervisors may always be referred to by clients as the out-group, and only clients can be members of the in-group. For the purposes of service-learning, it is difficult to figure out what are the rules of the groups, and how you will fit into the happenings of the site, but it is helpful to know that there may be groups there that are set up before you arrive, and those groups are very slow to change. It is difficult to change membership from one group to another, and because it is difficult, you may not be accepted as a group member, but you also do not need to be. You can learn from an insider what it is like to be in the group, and you can learn from others some of what you need to know about the site without being invited to actually being a member of the in-group. It should be understood as an objective status, rather than a personal affront to you. This is how communication pathways are necessary. If a site supervisor or faculty advisor can give you some information, you can then be informed of the different forms of communication that occur at the site commonly, and are considered acceptable.

Treating people negatively based on their culture can stem from ethnocentrism, which is assuming that your own culture, or ways of doing things, is superior to the culture of others. An ethnocentric outlook can easily lead to a sense of "us" versus "them," and when this type of outlook frames interactions it can lead to the use of language or name calling to justify treating "them" differently, and with inequality. In the past, certain forms of language have been used to indicate ethnocentricism, which can lead to the subjugation of people, such as in the case of the Native American being referred to as a "savage." This is best avoided by assuming your culture is not superior as much as it is a different way of life. *Difference* and *not superiority* are at the focus of this type of discussion. For the service-learner, the important message is to try to make sure that the relationships that you form through the project do not fail because of the lack of understanding that happens when two people from different cultures, or with different ages, or with different ability levels meet. If you both have a different way of shaking hands, or opposing views on religion, and if the other person does not respond as you anticipated, try not to let those symbolic gestures get in the way of a mutually beneficial relationship in which you can both ultimately learn from one another. This is not always easy, but is a worthwhile goal.

It may also help to prepare yourself in advance and know that there may be events that occur, or interactions will help you to discover something opposite from what you expected. There can always be unanticipated consequences, and those consequences may be in contradiction to your world view. For example, if we examine again the case of the person who would not shake your hand, when s/he did not shake your hand, that was likely to be viewed by you as unexpected and you interpreted it negatively, and thought that the person was rejecting you. If you told the person s/he was rude, then the other person would be upset, but the actual encounter would remain unchanged in that his or her behavior would remain the same and s/he would probably still not shake hands with strangers. Again, the best strategy would be to acknowledge that unanticipated consequences happen, and when you react to them, they might not necessarily alter a person's response. One instructive technique to use is to reflect on it, write about it descriptively, and learn from the situation. Also, you can acknowledge that these lessons can be life-changing in that your preconceived notions can be changed for a lifetime.

The service-learner can also pay attention to how s/he is making sense of the situation at the site, and how that sense-making affects the situation. People have a few sense-making techniques that they use to process the information they receive at the site. It is common for people to categorize one another, or to place people in specific groups such as white/black, disabled/nondisabled, in order to organize the vast amounts of information that they are confronted with in a new social situation. Frequently, service-learners do not have all the information that they need to come to an accurate categorization. For instance, if a service-learner is in a situation in which s/he is tutoring a child, but the child is not doing her homework, the service-learner may be in a situation in which s/he believes that the child is inept. With the proper context to the situation, the service-learner might discover the child is the sole provider for her family, and cannot do her homework because she is too busy. This is the type of situation that means the person who is doing the categorizing does not have adequate contextual information. It is also possible that the person who is categorized will also be attributed with certain characteristics that may or may not be correct or proper to the person. For instance, in the case of the tutored child, she could be given the status of lazy or lacking intelligence when the context would indicate that she is overworked.

One of the best recommendations when dealing with categorizing and miscommunication is to realize conflict is surmountable and is an occurrence that can be analyzed. As you write about an event you can also relive it, and reanalyze it in order to discover whether or not a conflictual situation was based on your own assumptions about how the other people involved should or should not act. While writing is an effective technique, it is also helpful to note that you can seek out commonalities instead of focusing on differences between individuals, and when you find that common ground, you can also establish a more secure and equal foundation for your service-learning relationship.

Having all the right information is also a helpful recommendation but it is not always possible for a service-learner to know the cultural pattern of the group prior to the service-learning visit. What is important to know is that when there are differences in the process of socialization there can be strong responses from a person who meets a foreign pattern of communication or interaction. If there is some conflict, you can anticipate those responses in advance. If there is initial conflict it is still very likely that you can communicate with others successfully, and find common ground with site supervisors, clients, or the other service-learners on your team. As different as cultural patterns may be, and despite initially experiencing some feelings of "differentness," we can also eventually relax with each other, learn from one another, and share common experiences with many types of people.

In addition to being prepared emotionally for some differences between service-learners in your group, clients, and site supervisors, another suggestion is to seek out someone who can give you the "insider perspective." It is possible that there is someone at the site who can educate you on what to expect in terms of different values and roles across cultural perspectives which are found at the community-based organization. If there is someone at the site who feels comfortable discussing topics with you, feel free to openly discuss these intercultural differences with him/her so s/he can shed some light on what issues are significant there, and what are good topics to discuss with others. It may be helpful to find out from an insider, what the customs are of the site, or what is done on a daily basis there. The best advice is to assume nothing, and discover what you can from working at the site, and gaining the insider perspective when you can, and when it seems the most comfortable for the clients and for the site supervisors.

It is important for service-learners to actively seek to communicate with one another, the factors that are important from their own cultural perspective. The point is to seek greater knowledge, and more of a global perspective on customs and ways of life, and to make sure that others do not feel that they have to defend their entire culture. Establishing a common ground does not necessarily imply emphasizing one culture as dominant over the other, or trying to extinguish differences, we can appreciate each other's differences while still discovering commonalities.

The following guidelines summarizes some of the points that have been written about diversity thus far in this manual, but in a more abbreviated form, and it also adds some recommendations on the best ways to handle intercultural communication:

### Ten Basic Rules of Intercultural Effectiveness
To improve relations with others, observe the following rules:

1. **Give people the benefit of the perceptual doubt. Assume goodwill.** This rule assumes that most individuals seek psychological comfort and congeniality.
2. **Minimize confrontations** by asking questions such as, "How's that?" and "How so?" Or say, "Please help me to understand why you see A or B the way you do." Here the emphasis is on giving the "other" an opportunity to explain his or her point of view.
3. **Ask for clarification.** "Would you please give me an example of A or B?" or "I'm not sure I understand what you mean, would you elaborate further?"
4. **Use "I" instead of "you" to deflect blame.** Say, "I'm having some difficulty understanding A or B" rather than "You are not explaining the origins of chopsticks very well."
5. **Try to look at people as individuals rather than as members of ethnic groups.** Some stereotyping will occur, of course, since we generally do not start each encounter with a clean slate of impressions.
6. **Seek common ground.** Learn about things that you share in common with others. For example, "My friend Yoshiko and I both love the musical group Hootie and the Blowfish."
7. **Be flexible in selecting words and actions.** Learn how to respond positively to conditions, people, and situations as they arise.
8. **Learn how to distinguish between things** that happen to you **because** you are white, Latino, Chinese, male or female, and things that happen to you in spite of your sex or ethnicity.
9. **Recognize the fact that people communicate differently.** For example, some people smile a lot; others do not.
10. **Develop empathy.** Try to infer the feelings and actions of others.

Calloway-Thomas, C. Cooper, P. J. & Blake, C. *Intercultural Communication: Roots and Routes* ©1999 by Allyn & Bacon. Reprinted/adapted by permission.

Learning about diversity by getting involved in service-learning projects is both challenging and rewarding. The service-learners will be involved in experiences that test their level of self-awareness to a greater extent than few other college courses can. It will teach you to confront your expectations, and to evaluate how those expectations affect what you observe, and how you interpret actions. Even when basic emotions are aroused, the service-learner will be confronted with dealing with those emotions, and trying to adapt himself or herself to what may seem like conflictual situations. Typical ways to react to situations based on one's own cultural patterns are challenged and the service-learner is called to speak to the challenge of finding solutions quickly. The service-learner will be doing and learning at the same time by juggling the in-group/out-group interpersonal actions and strategizing in order to find the insider's perspective.

Surprises and events that are counterintuitive can occur while involved in a service-learning project. While basic assumptions are being questioned, the service-learners will be asked to assume little and question much. By assuming little, the service-learner can make sense of new situation while exploring new solutions. The challenge will be to see a situation in a new light with an open mind and act as naive as possible, and realize that you have to think fast and strategize quickly in order to take command of all the action. While the service-learner learns about self, communication, negotiation, cultural patterns, and unanticipated consequences, s/he also knows that with all these challenges, s/he is reaping many rewards and finding something not everyone can discover: common ground in new territories.

# REFERENCES

Baker, P. (1980). Inquiry into the Teaching-Learning Process: Trickery, Folklore, or Science? *Teaching Sociology.* 7, 237–245.

Bellah, R., et al. (1985). *Habits of the Heart: Individualism and Commitment In American Life.* Berkeley: University of California Press.

Blau, J. (1999). Service-Learning: Not Charity, But a Two-Way Street. In J. Ostrow, et al. (Eds.), pp. ix–xv, *Cultivating the Sociological Imagination.* Washington, D.C.: American Association for Higher Education.

Boyer, E. (1987). College: *The Undergraduate Experience In America.* New York; Harper and Row.

Bringle, R., et al. (Eds.). (1999). *Colleges and Universities as Citizens.* Needham Heights: Allyn and Bacon.

Bringle, R. and J. A. Hatcher. (1995). A Service-Learning Curriculum for Faculty. *Michigan Journal of Community Service Learning.* 2, 112–122.

Calderon, J. and B. Farrell. (1996). Doing Sociology: Connecting the Classroom Experience With a Multi-ethnic School District. *Teaching Sociology.* 24, 46–53.

Calloway-Thomas, C., et al. (1999). *Intercultural Communication: Roots and Routes.* Needham Heights: Allyn and Bacon.

Chambliss, W. (1997). "The Saints and the Roughnecks." In D. Newman (Ed.), pp. 135–144, *Sociology: Exploring the Architecture of Everyday Life Readings.* Thousand Oaks: Pine Forge Press.

Cohen, L. (1995). Facilitating the Critique of Racism and Classism: An Experiential Model for Euro-American Middle-Class Students. *Teaching Sociology.* 23, 97–93.

Coleman, J. (1976). "Differences Between Experiential and Classroom Learning." In M. Keeton (Ed.), pp. 49–61, *Experiential Learning.* San Francisco: Josey-Bass.

———. (1974). *Youth: Transition to Adulthood.* Chicago: University of Chicago Press.

Coles, R. (1993). *The Call of Service: A Witness to Idealism.* Boston: Houghton Mifflin Co.

Corwin, P. (1996). Using the Community As A Classroom for Large Introductory Sociology Classes. *Teaching Sociology.* 24, 310–315.

Cushner, K. (1996). Human Diversity in Education: An Integrative Approach. New York: McGraw Hill.

Cushner, K. (1994). "Preparing Teachers for an Intercultural Context." In R. Brislin and T. Yoshida (Eds.), pp. 109–128, *Improving Intercultural Interactions: Modules for Cross-Cultural Training Programs,* Thousand Oaks: Sage Publications.

Dewey, J. (1952). *Experience and Education.* New York: Macmillan Co.

Dyer, W. (1995). *Team Building: Current Issues and New Alternatives.* Reading: Addison-Wesley.

Eby, J. (1998). "Why Service-Learning is Bad." Unpublished manuscript.

Ender, M., et al. (Eds.). (1996). *Service-Learning and Undergraduate Sociology: Syllabi and Instructional Materials.* The American Sociological Association.

Eyler, J., et al. (1996). *A Practitioner's Guide to Reflection in Service Learning: Student Voices and Reflections.* Nashville: Vanderbilt University.

Etzioni, A. (1993). *The Spirit of Community.* New York: Crown Publishers.

Everett, K. (1996). Social Inequality Syllabus. In Ender, et al. (Eds.), pp. 143, *Cultivating the Sociological Imagination.* Washington, D.C.: American Association for Higher Education.

Freire, P. (1973). *Education for Critical Consciousness.* New York: Continuum.

———. (1985). *The Politics of Education: Culture, Power, and Liberation.* New York: Bergin and Garvey.

Gondolf, E. (1980). Learning in the Community: An Undergraduate Training Program. *Teaching Sociology.* 7, 127–140.

Hondagneu-Sotelo, P. and S. Raskoff. (1994). Community Service-Learning: Promises and Problems. *Teaching Sociology.* 22, 248–254.

Jacoby, B. (1996). "Service-Learning in Today's Higher Education." In Jacoby, et al. (Eds.), pp. 3–25. *Service-Learning in Higher Education: Concepts and Practices.* San Francisco: Josey-Bass Publishers.

Jandt, F. E. (1998). *Intercultural Communication: An Introduction*. Thousand Oaks: Sage Publications.

Jorgensen, D. (1989). *Participation Observation: A Methodology for Human Sciences*. Newbury Park: Sage Publications.

Luce, J. et al. (1988). *Service Learning: An Annotated Bibliography Linking Public Service with the Curriculum*. Raleigh, NC: National Society for Experiential Education.

Lynch, E. W. and Hanson, M. J. (1998). *Developing Cross-Cultural Competence: A Guide for Working with Children and Their Families*. Baltimore: Paul H. Brookes Publishing Company.

Lynd, H. (1945). *Field Work in College Education*. New York: Columbia University Press.

Markwood, S. R. (1994). Volunteers in Local Government: Partners In Service. *Public Management*. 76:6.

Marullo, S. (1999). Sociology's Essential Role. In J. Ostrow, et al. (Eds.), pp. 11–27, *Cultivating the Sociological Imagination: Concepts and Models for Service-Learning in Sociology*. Washington, D.C.: American Association for Higher Education.

———. (1996). Community Involvement Seminar Syllabus. In Ender, et al. (Eds.), pp. 58, *Service-Learning and Undergraduate Sociology: Syllabi and Instructional Materials*. The American Sociological Association.

McEwen, M. K. (1996). Enhancing Student Learning and Development Through Service Learning. In Jacoby, et al. (Eds.), pp. 3–25. *Service-Learning in Higher Education: Concepts and Practices*. San Francisco: Josey-Bass Publishers.

Mintz, S. D. and G. W. Hesser. (1996). Principles of Good Practice in Service-Learning. In Jacoby, et al. (Eds.), pp. 3–25. *Service-Learning in Higher Education: Concepts and Practices*. San Francisco: Josey-Bass Publishers.

Newman, D. (1997). *Sociology: Exploring the Architecture of Everyday Life*. Thousand Oaks: Pine Forge Press.

Northcraft, G., Polzer, J., Neale, M., and Kramer, R. (in press). Diversity, Social Identity, and Performance: Emergent Social Dynamics in Cross-Functional Teams. In S. E. Jackson and M. N. Ruderman (Eds.), *Work Team Diversity: Paradigms and Perspectives*. Washington, D.C.: American Psychological Association.

Rhoads, R. (1997). *Community Service and Higher Learning: Explorations of the Caring Self*. Albany: State University of New York Press.

Rothman, M. (Ed). (1998). Service Matters: Engaging Higher Education in the Renewal of America's Communities and American Democracy. Providence: Campus Compact.

Schatzman, L. and A. Strauss. (1973). Field Research: Strategies for a Natural Sociology. Englewood Cliffs: Prentice-Hall.

Singelis, T. (1994). Nonverbal Communication. In R. Brislin and T. Yoshida (Eds.), pp. 268–294, *Improving Intercultural Interactions: Modules for Cross-Cultural Training Programs*. Thousand Oaks: Sage Publications.

Strand, K. (1999). Sociology and Service-Learning. In J. Ostrow, et al. (Eds.), pp. 29–37, *Cultivating the Sociological Imagination*. Washington, D.C.: American Association for Higher Education.

United States Department of Education. (1995). National Center for Education Statistics. *Profile of Undergraduates in United States Postsecondary Education Institutions: 1992–1993,* NCES 96-237, by Laura Horn and Mark Premo. Project Officer: Andrew G. Malizio. Washington D.C.

United States Department of Education. (1998). National Center for Education Statistics. *Profile of Undergraduates in U.S. Postsecondary Education Institutions: 1995–96,* NCES 98-084, by Laura J. Horn and Jennifer Berktold. Project officer: Andrew G. Malizio. Washington, D.C.

Watters, A. and M. Ford. (1995). *A Guide For Change: Resources For Implementing Community Service Writing*. New York: McGraw-Hill.

Zlotkowski, E. (Ed.). (1998). *Successful Service-Learning Programs*. Bolton: Anker Publishing Company.

# WEBSITES IN THE SERVICE-LEARNING FIELD

ACE Membership Department
One Dupont Circle, NW
Washington, DC 20036; Phone: 202-939-9336
Email: membership@ace.nche.edu
URL: **http://www.acenet.edu/**

The American Council on Education (ACE), founded in 1918, is the nation's coordinating higher education association. ACE is dedicated to the belief that equal educational opportunity and a strong higher education system are essential cornerstones of a democratic society. Its approximately 1,800 members include accredited, degree-granting colleges and universities from all sectors of higher education and other education and education-related organizations. ACE is a forum for the discussion of major issues related to higher education and its potential to contribute to the quality of America life. ACE maintains both a domestic and an international agenda and seeks to advance the interests and goals of higher and adult education in a changing environment by providing leadership and advocacy on important issues, representing the views of the higher and adult education community to policy makers, and offering services to its members.

Action Without Borders, Inc.
350 Fifth Avenue, Suite 6614
New York, NY 10118; Phone: 212-843-3973
Fax: 212-564-3377; Email: info@idealist.org
URL: **http://www.idealist.org/**

Action Without Borders is a global coalition of individuals and organizations working to build a world where all people can live free, dignified, and productive lives. Action Without Borders focuses on five goals from which everyone can benefit and to which anyone can contribute: promoting action and participation around the world; sharing ideas, experience and information; expanding the pool of resources available for good work; facilitating collaboration among individuals, organizations, schools, businesses, and other institutions; promoting the freedom to do all this. Action Without Borders is independent of any government, political ideology, or religious creed. Its work is guided by the common desire of its members and supporters to find practical solutions to social and environmental problems in a spirit of generosity and mutual respect.

America Reads Challenge
U.S. Department of Education
400 Maryland Avenue, SW
Washington, DC 20202-0107; Phone: 202-401-8888
Fax: 202-260-8114; Email: AmericaReads@ed.gov
URL: **http://ed.gov/inits/americareads/**

The America Reads Challenge is a grassroots national campaign that challenges every American to help all our children learn to read, including English Language Learners and students with disabilities. America Reads sparks collaborations between educators, parents, librarians, business people, senior citizens, college students, and community and religious groups.

America's Promise—The Alliance for Youth
909 North Washington Street, Suite 400
Alexandria, VA 22314-1556; Phone: 703-684-4500
Fax: 703-535-3900; Email: commit@americaspromise.org
URL: **http://www.americaspromise.org/**

America's Promise—The Alliance for Youth led by General Colin Powell, is dedicated to mobilizing individuals, groups, and organizations from every part of American life to build and strengthen the character and competence of our youth. It is a national organization dedicated to mobilizing the nation to ensure our children and youth have access to the fundamental resources they need to become successful adults.

American Association of Community Colleges
One Dupont Circle, NW, Suite 410
Washington, DC 20036; Phone: 202-728-0200
Fax: 202-833-2467
URL: **http://www.aacc.nche.edu/initiatives/service/service.htm**

The American Association of Community Colleges' service-learning initiative began with a 1994 grant from the Corporation for National Service to strengthen the service-learning infrastructure within and across community colleges, and to help train faculty members in skills needed to develop effective service-learning opportunities. AACC's objectives for its 1997–2000 Learn and Serve America project, Community Colleges Broadening Horizons through Service Learning, are to build support for and promote the concept and practice of service-learning, through presentations, print and electronic media, model programs, and training and technical assistance.

American Association of Higher Education Service-Learning Project
One Dupont Circle, Suite 360
Washington, DC 20036-1110; Phone: 202-293-6440
Fax: 202-293-0073; info@aahe.org
URL: **http://www.aahe.org/service/srv-lrn.htm**

The American Association of Higher Education Service Learning Project consists of a two-part initiative dedicated to the integration of service-learning across the disciplines. The project is anchored by an 18-volume series designed to provide resources to faculty wishing to explore community-based learning in and through the individual academic disciplines.

American Friends Service Committee
1501 Cherry Street
Philadelphia, PA 19102; Phone: 215-241-7000
Fax: 215-241-7275; Email: afscinfo@afsc.org
URL: **http://www.afsc.org/**

The American Friends Service Committee is a practical expression of the faith of the Religious Society of Friends (Quakers). Committed to the principles of nonviolence and justice, it seeks in its work and witness to draw on the transforming power of love, human and divine. They recognize that the leadings of the Spirit and the principles of truth found through Friends' experience and practice are not the exclusive possession of any group. Thus, the AFSC draws into its work people of many faiths and backgrounds who share the values that animate its life and who bring to it a rich variety of experiences and spiritual insights. The AFSC community works to transform conditions and relationships both in the world and in themselves which threaten to overwhelm what is precious in human beings. They nurture the faith that conflicts can be resolved nonviolently, that enmity can be transformed into friendship, strife into cooperation, poverty into well-being, and injustice into dignity and participation. They believe that ultimately goodness can prevail over evil, and oppression in all its many forms can give way.

American Red Cross
Attn: Public Inquiry Office
431 18th Street
Washington, DC 20006; Phone: 202-639-3520
URL: **http://www.redcross.org/volunter/vol.html**

The American Red Cross, a humanitarian organization led by volunteers and guided by its Congressional Charter and the Fundamental Principles of the International Red Cross Movement, will provide relief to victims of disasters and help people prevent, prepare for, and respond to emergencies.

AmeriSpan Unlimited
P.O. Box 40007, Philadelphia, PA 19106-0007
Phone: 800-879-6640; Fax: 215-751-1986
Email: info@amerispan.com
URL: **http://www.amerispan.com/**

AmeriSpan specializes in Spanish Immersion, Volunteer/Intern and Educational Travel programs throughout Mexico, the Caribbean, Central America, South America, and Spain. They are neither a language school nor a travel agent. They are a hybrid of the two, an educational travel company. They offer unbiased evaluations of all their programs because they are an independent company working as liaison between you and qualified language institutes throughout the Spanish-speaking world.

AmeriSpan sends thousands of people of all ages to participate in Spanish language immersion programs throughout Latin America and Spain. They recognize that each individual has different needs and expectations, therefore they offer a wide variety of programs.

Association for Experiential Education
2305 Canyon Boulevard, Suite #100
Boulder, CO 80302; Phone: 303-440-8844
Fax: 303-440-9581
URL: **http://www.aee.org/**

The mission of the Association for Experiential Education is to develop and promote experiential education in all settings. The Association is committed to support professional development, theoretical advancement, and evaluation in the field of experiential education worldwide.

> Casa Xelaju
> P.O. Box 3275, Austin, TX 78764-3275
> Phone: 512-416-6991; Fax: 512-416-8965
> Email: info@casaxelaju.com
> URL: **http://www.casaxelaju.com/**

Casa Xelajú (shay-la-hoo') is a socially-responsible educational institute in Quetzaltenango, Guatemala promoting cross-cultural understanding through its Spanish, Quiche languages and cultural programs, social projects, internship program, volunteer work, and travel services.

> Center for Intergenerational Learning at Temple University
> 1601 North Broad Street, Room 206
> Philadelphia, PA 19122; Phone: 215-204-6970
> Email: dlogan00@nimbus.temple.edu
> URL: **http://www.temple.edu/CIL/**

The Center for Intergenerational Learning at Temple University was created in 1980 to foster intergenerational cooperation and exchange. Through the development of innovative cross-age programs, the provision of training and technical assistance, and the dissemination of materials, the Center serves as a national resource for intergenerational programming.

> Explorations in Travel
> 1922 River Road
> Guilford, VT 05301; Phone: 802-257-0152
> Email: explore@sover.net
> URL: **http://www.exploretravel.com/**

Provides volunteer work placements for students and adults interested in spending an extended amount of time in an area, working on a foreign language, developing skills that will help in future employment, or just wanting a new, challenging experience. Placements can be arranged in Australia, New Zealand, Costa Rica, Puerto Rico, Mexico, Ecuador, and the U.S.

> Generations Together; University Center for Social and Urban Research
> University of Pittsburgh
> 121 University Place, Suite 300
> Pittsburgh, PA 15260-5907; Phone: 412-648-7150
> Email: johnani+@pitt.edu
> URL: **http://www.pitt.edu/~gti/service/index.htm**

Building an Intergenerational Service-Learning Infrastructure in Gerontology. The Association for Gerontology in Higher Education (AGHE) recognizes intergenerational service-learning as an innovative method of teaching and learning that fits naturally into the philosophy and pedagogy of aging education. Intergenerational service-learning provides students with direct contact with the aging community. It address the issues affecting this growing population, such as working to reduce stereotypes and to recognize the need to increase interest in working with older adults. Through an intergenerational service-learning project, students will improve their abilities to work with elders and to recognize their contributions to society.

Kids Can Make A Difference
P.O. Box 54
Kittery Point, ME 03905; Phone: 207-439-9588
Email: kids@kids.maine.org
URL: **http://www.kids.maine.org/**

Kids Can Make A Difference® (KIDS), an educational program for middle- and high-school students, focuses on the root causes of hunger and poverty, the people most affected, solutions, and how students can help. The major goal is to stimulate the students to take some definite follow-up actions as they begin to realize that one person can make a difference.

National Coalition for the Homeless
1012 Fourteenth Street, NW, #600
Washington, DC 20005-3410
Fax: 202-737-6445; Phone: 202-737-6444
Email: nch@ari.net
URL: **http://www.nch.ari.net/**

The National Coalition for the Homeless mission is to end homelessness. Toward this end, the National Coalition for the Homeless (NCH) engages in public education, policy advocacy, and grassroots organizing. NCH staff provide information to thousands of people each year, including practitioners, community groups, researchers, government staff, the general public, and the media. They publish reports and fact sheets, field many calls, and speak at conferences and workshops around the country. NCH maintains an extensive and constantly growing database on research, and responds to numerous inquiries. NCH publishes fact sheets on various aspects of homelessness, as well as an annotated bibliography, The Essential Reference on Homelessness: An Annotated Bibliography. NCH highlights new reports and research on homelessness in every issue of Safety Network, the newsletter of the National Coalition for the Homeless. Other public education projects include the Art and Literature project, the Educational Rights Project, and the Homeless Voices Project.

National Student Campaign Against Hunger and Homelessness (NSCAHH)
Julie Miles, Director
11965 Venice Blvd., Suite 408
Los Angeles, CA 90066; Phone: 1-800-NO-HUNGR ext. 324
Email: nscah@aol.com
URL: **http://www.pirg.org/nscahh/index.htm**

The National Student Campaign Against Hunger and Homelessness (NSCAHH) works with a coalition of students and community members across the country to end hunger and homelessness through education, service, and action. Started a decade ago by the PIRGs and USA for Africa, NSCAHH is now the largest student network fighting hunger and homelessness in the country, with more than 600 participating campuses in 45 states.

In the past fifteen years, they have helped many campuses organize Hunger and Homelessness Awareness Weeks; held annual conferences to bring hundreds of students and administrators together to learn about the issues and share project ideas; established Food Salvage programs to provide surplus cafeteria and restaurant food to food banks and shelters; developed Project Partnership to build community and campus coalitions; organized political efforts; and, through the Annual Hunger Cleanup, involved some 100,000 volunteers in service projects to raise more than $1 million for domestic and international relief.

> Oxfam America
> 76 West Street
> Boston, MA 02111; Phone: 800-77-OXFAM or 617-482-1211
> Fax: 617-728-2594; Email: info@oxfamamerica.org
> URL: **http://www.oxfamamerica.org/**

Oxfam America is dedicated to creating lasting solutions to hunger, poverty, and social injustice through long-term partnerships with poor communities around the world. As a privately funded organization, they speak with conviction and integrity as they challenge the structural barriers that foster conflict and human suffering and limit people from gaining the skills, resources, and power to become self-sufficient. Oxfam America supports the self-help efforts of poor and marginalized people—landless peasants, indigenous peoples, women, refugees, and survivors of war and natural disasters—striving to better their lives. Since 1970, Oxfam America has disbursed more than $100 million in program funding and technical support to hundreds of partner organizations in Africa, Asia, the Caribbean, and the Americas, including the United States.

Oxfam America also provides emergency aid when disaster strikes, assisting refugees and survivors of natural disasters. To the extent possible, Oxfam's partners use relief aid to address long-term development needs and prepare for future emergencies. In order to foster an environment where sustainable development can thrive, Oxfam America encourages the U.S. government and multilateral bodies to adopt policies that support, rather than hinder, long-term development.

From a simple humanitarian impulse in 1970, Oxfam America has built a solid foundation of private funding that has enabled it to develop and sustain a rich network of partnerships in some 30 countries. Oxfam has been a leader in shaping a concept of partnership that, in its essence, has become the ideal for other international aid organizations. Oxfam's annual Fast for World Harvest remains one of the largest anti-hunger campaigns in the United States.

> Clearinghouse for Service-Learning Organizations, Networks and Resources
> URL: **http://csf.colorado.edu/sl/**

Includes calendar of Service-Learning conferences, a guide to University Programs, Courses, Syllabi, and an electronic discussion group. A terrific resource to discover a wide range of service-learning organizations. Serves as a direct link to many other resources.

> Do Something
> 423 West 55th Street
> 8th Floor
> New York, NY 10019
> Phone: 212-523-1175; Fax: 212-582-1307
> Email: mail@dosomething.org
> URL: **http://dosomething.org/**

Do Something inspires young people to believe that change is possible, and they train, fund, and mobilize them to be leaders who measurably strengthen their communities.

America's Second Harvest
116 S. Michigan Ave., #4
Chicago, IL 60603
Phone: 312-263-2303
URL: **http://secondharvest.org**

Although it may be difficult to imagine, the best estimates place approximately 30 million Americans in danger of going hungry. These Americans are men, women, and children who don't know where they will get their next meal. From the ever-present needs of those living in poverty to the unexpected needs of those affected by natural disasters, Second Harvest is ready to help. Second Harvest is the largest charitable hunger relief organization in the United States. Our mission is to feed hungry people by soliciting and distributing food and grocery products through a nationwide network of certified affiliate food banks and to educate the public about the nature of and solutions to the problem of domestic hunger. The Second Harvest network of 189 regional food banks serves all 50 states and Puerto Rico, and distributes more than one billion pounds of donated food and grocery products annually. The Second Harvest network supports approximately 50,000 local charitable agencies that operate more than 94,000 food programs, including food pantries, soup kitchens, women's shelters, Kids Cafes, and other local organizations that provide food assistance to more than 26 million hungry Americans, including eight million children and four million seniors each year.

Amigos de las Américas
International Office
5618 Star Lane
Houston, TX 77057; Phone: 800-231-7796
Fax: 713-782-9267; Email: info@amigoslink.org
URL: **http://www.amigoslink.org/**

Amigos de las Américas is an international, voluntary, nongovernmental, not-for-profit organization that, through service: provides leadership development opportunities for young people; promotes community health in Latin America; and facilitates cross-cultural understanding for the people of the Americas. For over 30 years, Amigos de las Américas has provided a unique opportunity for high school and college students in the United States to make a difference in the world. Through the unparalleled "AMIGOS experience" over 18,000 young volunteers have completed extensive leadership and language training programs that prepare them to spend a summer as volunteers in ongoing community health projects throughout Latin America. The program begins with an extensive experience-based training program in the U.S. and Latin America. Once trained, volunteers are assigned to ongoing health and environmental programs partnered with sponsoring agencies in the host countries. They typically live with families in small communities in rural and semi-urban areas and are supervised by more experienced volunteers and officials of the host agency. AMIGOS strives to become a multicultural organization by actively recruiting volunteers from diverse backgrounds. AMIGOS affords equal opportunity to qualified individuals without regard to race, color, religion, gender, or national origin.

The ASPIRA Association
National Office
1444 Eye Street N.W., Suite 800
Washington, DC 20005; Phone: 202-835-3600
Fax: 202-835-3613; E-mail: info@aspira.org
URL: **http://www.aspira.org/**

The ASPIRA Association, Inc. is the only national nonprofit organization devoted solely to the education and leadership development of Puerto Rican and other Latino youth. ASPIRA takes its name from the Spanish verb *aspirar,* "aspire." Since 1961 ASPIRA has pursued its mission of empowering the Latino community through the development of its youth. All of ASPIRA's goals and activities spring from one basic belief: Puerto Ricans and Latinos have the collective potential to move their community forward. ASPIRA looks at Latino youth and sees this potential; leaders waiting to emerge. With community-based offices in large cities of six states and Puerto Rico, ASPIRA's 500 staff members work with over 25,000 youth and their families each year to develop that potential. These are Aspirantes—those youth who will become educated, committed leaders for the community's future benefit. Since its founding, ASPIRA has provided a quarter of a million youths with the personal resources they need to remain in school and contribute to their community. Most mainland Puerto Rican leaders today were encouraged by ASPIRA during their adolescence.

Arizona State University
Phone: 480-965-3097
URL: **http://www.asu.edu/duas/servlearn/**

Links to Science and English tutoring pages as well as program information for Arizona State University.

URL: **http://www.asu.edu/duas/servlearn/english/**

Detailed information about the Arizona State University English tutoring offerings, information to prospective students, and registration information.

URL: **http://www.asu.edu/duas/servlearn/science/**

Detailed information about the Arizona State University Science and Math Service-Learning projects.

Baja Outreach
Betsy McEnerney, Director
482 W San Ysidro Blvd STE 2043
San Ysidro, CA 92173-2410; Phone: 619-428-4011
URL: **http://www.geocities.com/Baja/4643/**

Baja Outreach is dedicated to helping the disadvantaged Mexican children and youth reach their potential by providing an educational/recreational center and nutritional program in Colonia Tecolote, Tijuana, Mexico.

Big Brothers Big Sisters of America
230 North 13th Street
Philadelphia, PA 19107; Phone: 215-567-7000

Fax: 215-567-0394; Email: NATIONAL@BBBSA.ORG
URL: **http://www.bbbsa.org/**

Big Brothers Big Sisters of America, the oldest mentoring organization serving youth in the country, remains the leading expert in our field. BBBSA has provided one-to-one mentoring relationships between adult volunteers and children at risk since 1904. BBBSA currently serves over 100,000 children and youth in more than 500 agencies throughout all of the United States.

As they approach their 100th anniversary, they are working to fulfill their commitment to the landmark Presidents' Summit by doubling the number of children they serve nationwide, and to provide community service opportunities for Bigs and Littles, by the end of the year 2000. BBBSA will continue to grow while maintaining our high standards of excellence for America's youth.

Best Buddies International, Inc.
100 Southeast Second Street
Suite 1990
Miami, Florida 3313; Phone: 305-374-2233
Fax: 305-374-5305; Email: info@bestbuddies.org
URL: **http://www.bestbuddies.org/**

Best Buddies is a nonprofit organization dedicated to enhancing the lives of people with mental retardation by providing opportunities for one-to-one friendships and integrated employment. Founded in 1989 by Anthony K. Shriver, Best Buddies has grown from one chapter on one college campus to a vibrant, international organization involving 13,000 participants annually on more than 400 high school and college campuses in the United States, Canada, and Greece. More than 80,000 individuals have volunteered in our ten years of existence.

Even though Best Buddies has grown tremendously in its short existence, most of the country still lacks programs to help people with mental retardation become a part of mainstream society. Our goal is to bring Best Buddies to every corner of the United States in the next ten years. Best Buddies programs need to be active on every high school and college campus nationwide.

There are more than 7.5 million people with mental retardation in the United States and 250 million worldwide. Paired with the 14 million college students in the US and the 77 million college students worldwide, we can make a huge difference in the lives of so many. The challenge is astounding, but with the power of volunteers and the generosity of our donors, it is attainable.

The Bonner Foundation
10 Mercer Street
Princeton, NJ 08540; Phone: 609-924-6663
Fax: 609-683-4626; Email: info@bonner.org
URL: **http://www.bonner.org/**

Through sustained partnerships with colleges and congregations, the Corella and Bertram F. Bonner Foundation seeks to improve the lives of individuals and communities by helping meet the basic needs of nutrition and educational opportunity.

Break Away
1531 P St., NW
Suite LL
Washington, DC 20005; Phone: 202-265-1200 x110
Fax: 202-265-3241 Email: breakaway@alternativebreaks.com
URL: **http://www.alternativebreaks.com/**

An alternative break program places teams of college or high school students in communities to engage in community service and experiential learning during their summer, fall, winter, or spring breaks. Students perform short-term projects for community agencies and learn about issues such as literacy, poverty, racism, hunger, homelessness, and the environment. The objectives of an alternative break program are to involve college students in community-based service projects and to give students opportunities to learn about the problems faced by members of communities with whom they otherwise may have had little or no direct contact. Examples of trips students have organized are: tutoring migrant farmworkers in Florida, building homes in Appalachia, registering voters in rural Mississippi, and working with the homeless in Washington, D.C.

Break Away: the Alternative Break Connection is a nonprofit organization that serves as a national resource of information on alternative break programs. They provide key information on planning and running a quality break program to schools and community organizations in the Break Away network. Break Away's programs and services include training and special events, publications, membership opportunities, networking, and access to the SiteBank Catalog, a directory of community organizations that host alternative break programs across the country. Break Away was founded in June 1991 by Michael Magevney and Laura Mann, and is based at Vanderbilt University.

Catholic Network of Volunteer Service
4121 Harewood Road, NE,
Washington, DC 20017-1593
Phone: 1-800-543-5046
Fax: 202-526-1094
URL: **http://www.cnvs.org/**

Coordinates approximately 184 Catholic and Christian organizations which need volunteers. Long-term and short-term appointments available.

Community Action Network
URL: **http://www.getinvolved.net/**

Offers a wide range of services, from connecting volunteers with the needs in their community to an online database of organizations, donors, and volunteers. Type in your zip code and they'll match you with volunteer opportunities in your area.

Corporation for National Service
1201 New York Avenue, NW
Washington, DC 20525; Phone: 202-606-5000
Email: webmaster@cns.gov
URL: **http://www.americorps.org/**

AmeriCorps is the national service program through which 40,000 people each year tackle community problems from disaster relief to tutoring.

URL: **http://www.ccc.ca.gov/frame.htm**

The California Conservation Corps, or CCC, is an innovative state agency with a dual mission—the employment and development of youth, and the protection and enhancement of the state's natural resources. The CCC follows in the footsteps of the federal Civilian Conservation Corps of the 1930s. Today's California program, established in 1976, is the oldest and largest conservation corps now in operation. The CCC's organizational structure consists of northern and southern field divisions, with 11 districts and more than 30 satellite facilities located throughout the state. The CCC has been the model for youth corps programs on the local, state and national levels, and attracted inquiries and visitors from more than 45 foreign countries. Along with its day-to-day conservation work, the CCC has become known as one of California's premier emergency response forces. When floods, fires, oil spills, or earthquakes occur, the Corps can provide assistance within hours.

Christmas in April*USA
1536 Sixteenth Street, NW
Washington, DC 20036-1402
Phone: 202-483-9083
Fax: 202-483-9081; Email: general_mail@christmasinapril.org
URL: **http://www.christmasinapril.org/**

Christmas in April provides assistance to people who own their own home but who, because of physical limitation or income, are not able to cover the costs of home repair. Typically, these individuals have a disability and/or are elderly, but low-income families and nonprofit facilities such as schools, shelters, and daycare centers are also included. Christmas in April takes its cue from the old fashioned idea of "barn raising," with as many as 75 skilled and unskilled volunteers assigned to a particular project. Homeowners are frequently amazed at the sheer number of people who come out to lend them a helping hand. They are even more amazed at the massive amount of work that can be accomplished by caring volunteers in a short period of time.

Commission on Improving Life Through Service
1110 K Street, Suite 210
Sacramento, CA 95833
Phone: 916-323-7646
Fax: 916-323-3227
URL: **http://www.cilts.ca.gov/index.html**

The California Commission on Improving Life Through Service coordinates AmeriCorps*USA, a federal national service program, through a network of local area service partnerships, designed to address some of the state's most critical and persistent social epidemics. Local partnerships engage Americans of all ages, abilities, and backgrounds in getting things done throughout the nation's urban and rural communities.

City Year
285 Columbus Avenue
Boston, MA 02116
Phone: 617-927-2500
Fax: 617-927-2510
URL: **http://www.city-year.org/**

In his inaugural address, Thomas Menino, the mayor of Boston, called for City Year teams in every public school. To date, 31,701 school children across the nation have been served by City Year teams. Corps members serve as teachers aides and mentors. They run after-school programs, school vacation camps, conflict resolution workshops, and develop HIV/AIDS curricula. Mary Russo, the principal of Mason Elementary School, Roxbury, MA, says "City Year's presence has translated into more for the kids.... The partnership is a synergistic relationship. Both the Mason School and City Year brought particular strengths to the partnership. The two coalesced and produced something even better than the original plans. Every group in the school has been impacted."

Close Up Foundation
44 Canal Center Plaza
Alexandria, VA 22314-1592
Phone: 256-7387
URL: **http://www.closeup.org/**

Democracy is not a spectator sport—it requires the active participation of citizens. The Close Up Foundation is the nation's largest nonprofit, nonpartisan citizenship education organization. Since its founding in 1970, Close Up has worked to promote responsible and informed participation in the democratic process through a variety of educational programs.

Close Up's mission is built on the belief that textbooks and lectures alone are not enough to help students understand the democratic process and make it work. Students need a "close up" experience in government. Close Up's national, state, and local experiential government studies programs strengthen participants' knowledge of how the political process works, increase their awareness of major national and international issues, and motivate them to become actively involved in the world around them.

Close Up believes that all individuals deserve the opportunity to become fully engaged citizens of our democracy. At the Close Up Foundation, they strive to make their programs accessible for all citizens, regardless of age, race, or ability. The support the Foundation receives from foundations, corporations, individuals, and Congress allows Close Up to provide tuition fellowships for economically disadvantaged students. This assistance ensures that they, too, will understand the true meaning behind a democracy—that each citizen has a voice, and that each citizen's actions can make a difference.

Each year, more than 25,000 students, teachers, and other adults take part in Close Up's programs in Washington, D.C. Since the inception of its Washington-based programs in 1971, the Close Up Foundation has welcomed nearly 500,000 students, educators, and other adults to the nation's capital.

Tens of thousands more across the country participate in state and local government studies programs. The Close Up message of citizen participation reaches millions annually through award-winning publications, video productions, and national television programming.

Campus Compact
Box 1975
Brown University
Providence, RI 02912-1975
Phone: 401-863-1119
Fax: 401-863-3779; Email: campus@compact.org.
URL: **http://www.compact.org**

Campus Compact is a coalition of college and university presidents committed to helping students develop the values and skills of citizenship through participation in public and community service. It is the only national higher education organization whose primary purpose is to support campus-based public and community service.

Campus Outreach Opportunity League
1531 P Street NW, Suite LL
Washington, DC 20005; Phone: 202-265-1200
Fax: 202-265-3241; Email: homeoffice@COOL2SERVE.org
URL: **http://www.COOL2SERVE.org**

Founded in 1984, the Campus Outreach Opportunity League (COOL) is a national, non-profit organization dedicated to the education and empowerment of college students to strengthen our nation through community service. Their vision is to mobilize and connect students of all backgrounds to lead a movement that increases participation in our communities, promotes activism, and fosters the civic and social responsibility necessary to build a just society.

CARES
c/o Doug Ross
914 Old Lancaster Rd.
Bryn Mawr, PA 19010; Phone: 610-527-3539
Fax: 610-527-7469; Email: ssciinst@home.com
URL: **http://library.advanced.org/50017/**

CARES is a comprehensive course designed to enable teachers to implement community service learning projects, which will connect their students to each other and their communities, while they master important academic skills. The acronym CARES stands for Community, Activities, Resources, Environment and Service.

Center for Democracy and Citizenship
Hubert Humphrey Institute of Public Affairs
301 19th Avenue South
Minneapolis, MN 55455; Phone: 612-625-0142
Fax: 612-625-3513; Email: eeschenbacher@hhh.umn.edu
URL: **http://www.hhh.umn.edu/centers/cdc/**

The Center for Democracy and Citizenship at the Humphrey Institute had its beginnings in 1987, when then Dean Harlan Cleveland asked Harry Boyte to work on "problems of democracy." Concretely, they have taken this charge as the development of practical theory about "what works" to engage citizens in public life, to unleash and cultivate people's public talents, and to renew the public cultures and democratic purposes of service institutions. From the beginning, the Center has also kept in mind as well an overarching task: their goal is to participate with others in the public work of renewing and strengthening democracy—to make the idea of democracy as a commonwealth created and produced by the public work of citizens come alive once again, different than the "consumer democracy" that now dominates.

Creating and sustaining a vibrant democracy has been America's great nfinished work, a legacy and also an aspiration, both of which lend larger meaning to private lives and to civic institutions of all kinds. The Center for Democracy and Citizenship is convinced that democracy remains the urgent public task and the unrealized promise of the nation, at the threshold of the new millennium.

> The Center for Living Democracy
> 289 Fox Farm Road
> Brattleboro, VT 05301; Phone: 802-254-1234
> Fax: 802-254-1227
> URL: **http://www.livingdemocracy.org/**

The Center for Living Democracy Learning Center offers over 300 community-building resources in the Tool Box catalog and provides opportunities to bridge the racial divide through the Interracial Democracy program.

CLD's American News Service (ANS), the world's largest nonprofit newswire, was founded in 1995 to cover promising initiatives in education, the environment, health, crime and violence prevention, race relations, workplace conditions, and economic and community development—and more. ANS currently distributes ten new "solutions news" stories to media and others across the country every week.

> Civic Practices Network (CPN)
> Center for Human Resources
> Heller School for Advanced Studies in Social Welfare
> Brandeis University
> 60 Turner Street
> Waltham, MA 02154; Phone: 617-736-4890
> Fax: 617-736-4891; Email: cpn@tiac.net
> URL: **http://www.cpn.org/**

Born of the movement for a "new citizenship" and "civic revitalization," Civic Practices Network is a collaborative and nonpartisan project dedicated to bringing practical tools for public problem-solving into community and institutional settings across America. Their common mission is to tell the stories of civic innovation, share the practical wisdom, and exchange the most effective tools available. Their affiliates provide case studies from which others can learn. They provide training manuals, "best practice" guides, and evaluative tools so that all of them can become more skillful about the public work that they do. They map innovative projects around the country, and help each other locate other civic assets and partners. And they engage each other about the big ideas that underlie our democratic heritage so that they can continue to renew it to meet the challenges of the 21st century.

CPN is a pluralist and nonpartisan network of civic educators and practitioners who share this commitment. Their World Wide Web pages provide online, multimedia capacities to exchange the broadest range of practical tools and diverse experiences, and to fashion these for use in many different settings: schools and professional training programs, community centers and public libraries, government agencies and private businesses, homes and churches—wherever people gather to do important civic work and learning.

They provide these online to the broad public as a common resource for practical civic education, responsible community action, and democratic policy making. They can be printed out, photocopied, and assembled as customized workbooks, course readers, and resource guides. Original printed materials and other resources can be ordered from their affiliates, and previewed online: videos, manuals, audiotapes, project evaluations. CPN charges no fee for this service, and minimizes copyright barriers for all nonprofit educational uses.

> Constitutional Rights Foundation
> 601 South Kingsley Drive,
> Los Angeles, CA 90005; Phone: 213-487-5590
> Fax: 213-386-0459
> URL: **http://www.crf-usa.org/**

Constitutional Rights Foundation (CRF) is a nonprofit, nonpartisan, community-based organization dedicated to educating America's young people about the importance of civic participation in a democratic society. Under the guidance of a Board of Directors chosen from the worlds of law, business, government, education, the media, and the community, CRF develops, produces, and distributes programs and materials to teachers, students, and public-minded citizens all across the nation. CRF staff includes teachers and educators, lawyers and athletes, community organizers and fundraisers, designers, writers and editors. They provide technical assistance and training to teachers, coordinate civic participation projects in schools and communities, organize student conferences and competitions, and develop publications in the following areas: Law and Government programs and materials focus on how groups and individuals interact with the issues, institutions, people and processes that shape our laws and government. Civic Participation programs and materials bring to life the rights and responsibilities of active citizenship by challenging young people to explore their community and plan and implement projects that address community needs. Business in Society programs and materials focus on the role that business issues, ethics, and decision-making play in the social, economic, and civic life of our society.

> Council for Spiritual and Ethical Education
> 1465 Northside Drive, Suite 220
> Atlanta, GA 30318; Phone: 800-298-4599
> Fax: 404-355-4435; Email: info@csee.org
> URL: **http://www.csee.org/**

Council for Spiritual and Ethical Education understands the search for meaning as universal and essential, supports the search as necessary to the nourishment of young people of conscience and community. Serves as a national resource for schools to encourage the moral, ethical, and spiritual development of young people. Promotes community service, providing resources and a network for schools' involvement in community service and service-learning. Develops programs and services, which encourage a school climate of open ethical and religious inquiry and expression. Supports instruction in world religions and ethics as essential components of a complete education.

Department of Natural Resources
101 South Webster Street
Box 7921
Madison WI 53707-7921; Phone: 608-266-2621
Fax: 608-267-3579; Email: csweb@www.dnr.state.wi.us
URL: **http://dnr.state/wi.us**

These pages are designed to help educators teach Environmental Education for Kids. EEK! is an electronic magazine for kids in grades 4–8 and is sponsored by the Wisconsin Department of Natural Resources.

The EnviroLink Network
5808 Forbes Ave.
Second Floor
Pittsburgh, PA 15217; Phone: 412-420-6400
Fax: 412-420-6404; Email: support@envirolink.org
URL: **http://www.envirolink.org/**

EnviroLink is a nonprofit organization, a grassroots online community that unites hundreds of organizations and volunteers around the world with millions of people in more than 150 countries. EnviroLink is dedicated to providing the most comprehensive, up-to-date environmental resources available.

The EnviroLink Network was created in 1991 by Josh Knauer while he was a fresh-man at Carnegie Mellon University. Since that time, EnviroLink has grown from a simple mailing list of 20 student activists to become one of the world's largest environmental in-formation clearinghouses. In addition to being an information resource, EnviroLink pro-vides environmental nonprofits with website hosting, automated mailing lists, interactive bulletin boards and chat rooms, as well as other services. The majority of these services are provided free of charge to environmental organizations.

At EnviroLink they are committed to promoting a sustainable society by connecting individuals and organizations through new communications technologies. They recognize that our technologies are just tools, and that the solutions to our ecological challenges lie within our communities and their connection to the Earth itself. The organization does not take any positions on any environmental issues, it exists solely to act as a clearinghouse on the Internet for the environmental community, which is incredibly diverse in its views. En-viroLink is supported by the generosity of many environmentally conscious individuals, organizations, and corporations.

Earth Preservers
P.O. Box 6
Westfield, NJ 07090
URL: **http://earthpreservers.com**

The environmental newspaper for adults and children can add insight to environmen-tal service-learning projects.

Earthsystems.org: The source for environmental education
508 Dale Avenue
Charlottesville, Virginia 22903; Phone: 804-293-6398
URL: **http://www.earthsystems.org**

Earthsystems.org is a nonprofit 501(c)3 organization that develops, compiles, categorizes, and delivers environmental education and information resources to the world at large using leading electronic technologies.

Also find: **http://earthsystems.org/ways/**

54 Ways You Can Help The Homeless is written by Rabbi Charles A. Kroloff and the website is sponsored by Earthsystems. This on-line guide gives 54 suggestions on things people of any age can do to help the homeless. Although many of the suggestions refer to volunteer opportunities, with a little bit of adaptation they can be made into service-learning projects.

Earthwatch Institute
3 Clocktower Place, Suite 100
Box 75
Maynard, MA 01754; Phone (US/Can): 1-800-776-0188
Fax: 617-926-8532; Email: info@earthwatch.org
URL: **http://www.earthwatch.org/**

Earthwatch Institute is an international nonprofit organization, which supports scientific field research worldwide to improve our understanding and management of the Earth. The Institute's mission is to promote sustainable conservation of our natural resources and cultural heritage by creating partnerships between scientists, educators, and the general public. Through the participation of volunteers in field research, Earthwatch helps scientists gather vital data that empowers individuals and governments to act wisely as global citizens.

Earthwatch offers its 25,000 members worldwide the unusual opportunity to work side-by-side with distinguished field scientists in seven areas of global concern: Oceans; Endangered Ecosystems; Biodiversity; Cultural Diversity; Origins of our Future; Global Change; and World Health. In 1999, Earthwatch is sponsoring 115 projects in 48 countries and 19 of the United States. Whether it's studying dolphin behavior in New Zealand, indigenous herbal medicine in Kenya, or Pleistocene mammal fossils in Mexico, Earthwatch volunteers support field science in action where it is most needed. Each year, 4,000 participants join our field teams from the ranks of our membership. For most it is a life-changing experience that inspires them to do much more.

Since its founding in 1971, Earthwatch Institute has mobilized more than 1,500 projects around the globe. The findings from these projects have resulted in the discovery of 2,000 new species, the establishment of 12 national parks, and the founding of 8 museums. Earthwatch teams have brought medicine, clean water, and proper nutrition to remote villages of 20 countries. Whether Earthwatch members contribute to these results by volunteering in the field, or merely enjoy the colorful Research and Exploration Guide and Earthwatch magazines that are a benefit of membership, they believe they are a vital link to finding solutions for a sustainable future on Earth.

Echoing Green Foundation
198 Madison Avenue–8th floor
New York, NY 10016; Phone: 212-689-1165
Fax: 212-689-9010; Email: general@echoinggreen.org
URL: **http://www.echoinggreen.org/**

Echoing Green is a non-profit foundation that offers full-time fellowships to emerging social entrepreneurs. Their foundation applies a venture capital approach to philanthropy by providing seed money and technical support to individuals creating innovative public service organizations or projects that seek to catalyze positive social change. Echoing Green invests in entrepreneurs' organizations and projects at an early stage, before most funders are willing to do so, and then provides them with support to help them grow beyond start-up. The Echoing Green community currently includes over 300 Fellows working domestically and internationally on a wide range of social issues.

U.S. Department of Education
400 Maryland Avenue, SW
Washington, DC 20202; Phone: 1-800-USA-LEARN
Fax: 202-401-0689; Email: CustomerService@inet.ed.gov
URL: **http://www.ed.gov/Welcome/overview.html**

The Department of Education administers over 200 programs in order to:
1) provide national leadership and partnerships to address critical issues in American education; 2) serve as a national clearinghouse of good ideas; 3) help families pay for college; 4) help local communities and schools meet the most pressing needs of their students; 5) prepare students for employment in a changing economy; 6) ensure nondiscrimination by recipients of federal education funds.

Educational Resources Information Center (ERIC)
One Dupont Circle Suite #630
Washington, DC 20036, Phone: 800/773-3742
Fax: 202-452-1844.
URL: **http://www.eriche.org/**

The Educational Resources Information Center (ERIC) is a national information system designed to provide users with ready access to an extensive body of education-related literature. ERIC, established in 1966, is supported by the U.S. Department of Education, Office of Educational Research and Improvement, and the National Library of Education.

NSRC
ETR Associates
P.O. Box 1830
Santa Cruz, CA 95061-1830; Phone: 800-860-2684 or 831-438-4060
Fax: 831-430-9471; E-mail: nsrc@etr.org
URL: **http://www.etr-associates.org/NSRC/**

National Service Resource Center supports and serves the programs of Corporation for National Service "getting things done" in communities throughout the USA. These include AmeriCorps, AmeriCorps VISTA, AmeriCorps NCCC, National Senior Service Corps, Learn and Serve America, and America Reads. Their mission is to act as a central point for sharing and distribution of training and technical assistance information and resources.

The Foundation Center
79 Fifth Avenue
New York, NY 10003; Phone: 212-620-4230
Fax: 212-691-1828
URL: **http://www.fdncenter.org/**

The Foundation Center is an independent nonprofit information clearinghouse established in 1956. The Center's mission is to foster public understanding of the foundation field by collecting, organizing, analyzing, and disseminating information on foundations, corporate giving, and related subjects. The audiences that call on the Center's resources include grantseekers, grantmakers, researchers, policymakers, the media, and the general public.

Georgetown University
Volunteer and Public Service (VPS) Center
B-01 St. Mary's Hall
Washington, DC 20057; Phone: 202-687-3703
Email: vps@gunet.georgetown.edu
URL: **http://www.georgetown.edu/outreach/vps/**

The Volunteer and Public Service Center upholds the Jesuit mission to educate men and women for others by engaging Georgetown students, staff, and faculty in community-based work in order to deepen their understanding of community and social justice and to explore the link between service and academic theory.

Gonzaga University Center for Community Action and Service Learning
MSC 2472
502 East Boone
Spokane, WA 99258-2472; Phone: 509-323-6824
Email: thrope@gu.gonzaga.edu
URL: **http://www.gonzaga.edu/service/gvs/service_learning/**

The website for the service-learning office at Gonzaga University works closely with service-learning faculty and approximately 300 Gonzaga students who are involved in a myriad of service-learning projects each semester. Students are matched with agencies and projects carefully, meeting the needs of the faculty and the community as well as student interests.

The Higher Education Research Institute
Service-Learning Clearinghouse Project
2005C Moore Hall/Box 951521
Los Angeles, CA 90095-1521; Phone: 310-206-4815
Fax: 310-794-5004; Email: heslcp@gseis.ucla.edu
URL: **http://www.gseis.ucla.edu/slc/**

"Provide the higher education service-learning field with Higher Education Research Institute faculty and student research findings pertinent to the service-learning field."

The Holiday Project
104 Kingsland Road
Landing, NJ 07850; Phone: 973-770-6450
Fax: 973-770-6431 Email: sorresse@bellatlantic.net
URL: **http://www.holiday-project.org/**

The Holiday Project is a national nonprofit organization managed by volunteers who visit with people spending Christmas, Chanukah, and other holidays throughout the year confined in hospitals, nursing homes, shelters, prisons, and other institutions.

The Hunger Site
720 Olive Way, Suite 1800
Seattle, WA 98101
URL: **http://www.thehungersite.com/**

The Hunger Site was founded by a private individual as an independent and nonpartisan Internet site to help alleviate hunger in the world. It enables people to learn about hunger and to make free donations of food to the hungry. It is not owned by any company or affiliated with any group or organization—political, religious, or otherwise. All you do is click a button and somewhere in the world some hungry person gets a meal to eat at no cost to you. The food is paid for by corporate sponsors. All you do is go to the site and click. But you are only allowed one click per day. It is a creative and wonderful way to use the internet to benefit people throughout the world using the United Nations World Food Program.

The International Partnership for Service-Learning
815 Second Avenue, Suite 315
New York, NY 10017; Phone: 212-986-0989
Email: plsny@aol.com
URL: **http://www.studyabroad.com**

The on-line study abroad information resource. Includes listings for thousands of study abroad programs in more than 100 countries throughout the world. You will also find hundreds of links to study abroad program home pages and a wealth of related information.

The Internet Public Library
304 West Hall SEB
550 E. University
Ann Arbor, MI; 48109-1092; Phone: 734-764-4386
Fax: 734-764-2475; Email: ipl@ipl.org
URL: **http://www.ipl.org/**

The Internet Public Library is an educational initiative of the University of Michigan School of Information and is sponsored by Bell & Howell Information and Learning. Staffed by professional librarians with assistance from students and volunteer librarians from around the world, it has been visited by more than 7 million people from over 100 countries. The library maintains a collection of online ready reference works; responds to reference questions; creates web resources; evaluates and categorizes resources on the Internet; and provides a space for exhibits.

Partner Service Center
Habitat for Humanity International
121 Habitat St.
Americus, GA 31709; Phone: 912-924-6935, ext. 2551 or 2552
Email: public_info@habitat.org
URL: **http://www.habitat.org/**

Habitat for Humanity International is a nonprofit, ecumenical Christian housing ministry. HFHI seeks to eliminate poverty housing and homelessness from the world, and to make decent shelter a matter of conscience and action. Habitat invites people of all backgrounds, races, and religions to build houses together in partnership with families in need. Habitat has built more than 80,000 houses around the world, providing more than 400,000 people in more than 2,000 communities with safe, decent, affordable shelter. HFHI was founded in 1976 by Millard Fuller along with his wife Linda.

Through volunteer labor and donations of money and materials, Habitat builds and rehabilitates simple, decent houses with the help of the homeowner (partner) families. Habitat houses are sold to partner families at no profit, financed with affordable, no-interest loans. The homeowners' monthly mortgage payments are used to build still more Habitat houses.

Habitat is not a giveaway program. In addition to a down payment and the monthly mortgage payments, homeowners invest hundreds of hours of their own labor—"sweat equity"—into building their Habitat house and the houses of others.

Independent Sector
1200 Eighteenth Street
Suite 200
Washington, DC 20036; Phone: 202-467-6100
Fax: 202-467-6101; Email: info@IndependentSector.org
URL: **http://www.indepsec.org/**

Independent Sector is a national leadership forum, working to encourage philanthropy, volunteering, not-for-profit initiative, and citizen actionthat help us better serve people and communities.

Institute for Service-Learning
Henry Ave. and Schoolhouse Ln.
Philadelphia, PA 19144
Phone: 215-951-2564
Fax: 215-951-2128
Email: institute@philacol.edu
URL: **www.philacol.edu/institute**

The Atlantic Regional Center of the Learn and Serve America Exchange, led by the National Youth Leadership Council, supports service-learning programs in schools, colleges and universities, and community organizations across the country through peer-based training and technical assistance. If you need assistance implementing service-learning programs, have questions, or simply want to speak with someone who has "been there," you can utilize the Exchange as a resource.

Jumpstart National
93 Summer Street, 2nd Floor
Boston, MA 02110; Phone: 617-542-JUMP (5867)
Fax: 617-542-2557; Email: dave_ellis@jstart.org
URL: **http://www.jstart.org/**

Jumpstart engages young people in service to their community to work toward the day that every child in America will enter first grade prepared to succeed. To accomplish this mission, Jumpstart builds School Success, Family Involvement, and Future Teachers, one child at a time. College students who serve as Jumpstart Corps members work one-on-one with a young child for four hours every week to build vital literacy and learning skills. The children with whom the Corps members work are referred by their preschool teachers as children who could most benefit from additional one-on-one attention. Once the referral process has been completed, Corps members work in teams of 8 to 10 for two afternoons per week in preschool classrooms that would otherwise be unused during that time. The team of Corps members and the children they work with will stay together during the entire school year allowing a strong relationship to form that serves as the foundation for future learning.

> Kaboom! Headquarters
> 2213 M Street NW, Suite 300
> Washington, D.C. 20037
> Phone: 202-659-0215, ext. 225
> URL: **http://www.kaboom.org/**

This year, America will send more than 200,000 of its children to emergency rooms with serious injuries sustained from playground falls and other accidents. For too many of our children, playgrounds are not open spaces with safe, colorful equipment. Instead, they are garbage-strewn lots, abandoned cars, drain spouts filled with broken glass, bushes riddled with crack vials and needles, or boarded-up and abandoned buildings. Even for those families whose playgrounds appear safe, hidden dangers exist: inadequate surfacing; jagged equipment edges that can pinch and tear skin; outdated equipment that can catch drawstrings and choke children; and, simply, poorly maintained equipment.

Safe and accessible playgrounds are critical to the development of America's children. They provide a haven for children to play games with friends, keep fit and healthy, and develop social skills. Playgrounds also create excellent spaces for parents and grandparents to spend time with their children, and for neighbors to build vital social networks within their communities.

KaBOOM! is a national nonprofit organization that fosters those networks and provides those spaces for kids to grow. They inspire individuals, organizations, and businesses to join together to build much-needed, safe, and accessible playgrounds. Through this team effort, They help communities create a model of partnerships that achieves positive and sustainable changes in neighborhoods nationwide.

> Kids Care Clubs
> P.O. Box 1083
> New Canaan, CT 06840; Phone: 914-533-1101
> Fax: 914-533-2949; Email: kids.care@kidscare.org
> URL: **http://www.kidscare.org/kidscare/index.htm**

Our mission is to develop the spirit of compassion and volunteerism in children. To that end, we provide children, families, schools, and religious groups with meaningful opportunities to help others in their local and other communities. We call it "hands-on love."

Foundation for Individual Responsibility and Social Trust
2500 One Liberty Place
Philadelphia, PA 19103

OR

We the Future
430 Gladfelter Hall
1115 Berks St.
Philadelphia, PA 19122; Phone: 1-888-FIRST96 (toll free)
Fax: 215-204-3770; Email: first@libertynet.org
URL: **http://www.libertynet.org/~first**

The Foundation for Individual Responsibility and Social Trust (FIRST), is a nonpartisan, nonprofit organization dedicated to inspiring the generation of young adults to address the major political, economic, and social issues of our time at their most basic level while taking a leadership role in finding creative and positive outcomes.

Ed Schwartz, Institute for the Study of Civic Values
1218 Chestnut St., Rm. 702
Philadelphia, Pa. 19107; Phone: 215-238-1434
Fax: 215-238-0530; Email: edcivic@libertynet.org
URL: **http://www.libertynet.org/edcivic/iscvhome.html**

The Institute for the Study of Civic Values is a non-profit organization established in Philadelphia in 1973 to promote the fulfillment of America's historic civic ideals. At a time when millions of Americans are struggling to identify the values that we share, the Institute for the Study of Civic Values believes that it is our civic values—the principles embodied in the Declaration of Independence, the Constitution, and the Bill of Rights—that bring us together as a people. For more than 20 years in Philadelphia, the Institute has conducted a wide range of seminars, workshops, and public forums aimed at applying America's civic values to contemporary issues and problems. In the process, they have helped thousands of people and grassroots organizations gain the knowledge and skills needed for effective participation in the community and politics. They have received significant support from government, the private sector, and a wide range of private contributors for these efforts.

Literacy Volunteers of America
635 James Street
Syracuse, NY 13203-2214; Phone: 315-472-0001
Fax: 315-472-0002; Email: info@literacyvolunteers.org
URL: **http://www.literacyvolunteers.org/home/index.htm**

Literacy Volunteers of America, Inc. (LVA) is a national network of 366 locally based programs, supported by state and national staff. Their mission is to change lives through literacy. Professionally trained volunteer tutors teach Basic Literacy, and English for Speakers of Other Languages to courageous, motivated adults. Literacy skills enable

LVA students to be better parents, workers, and citizens. And their individual gains benefit their families, employers, and society.

> League of Women Voters
> 1730 M Street NW, Suite 1000
> Washington, DC 20036-4508; Phone: 202-429-1965
> Fax: 202-429-0854
> URL: **http://www.lwv.rg/**

The League of Women Voters, a nonpartisan political organization, encourages the informed and active participation of citizens in government, works to increase understanding of major public policy issues, and influences public policy through education and advocacy.

> Maricopa County Community College
> URL: **http://www.mc.maricopa.edu/academic/compact/**

Campus Compact is a membership organization which supports a burgeoning level of community service activity among students, faculty and administration on over 500 college and university campuses across the country. Campus Compact awarded Maricopa County Community College District a subgrant from ACTION, the federal volunteer agency, to establish a national technical assistance center. Thus, in November of 1990, the Campus Compact National Center for Community Colleges (CCNCCC) opened its doors at Mesa Community College.

> National Mentoring Partnership
> 1400 I Street, NW, Suite 850
> Washington D.C. 20005; Phone: 202-729-4345
> Fax: 202-729-4341
> URL: **http://www.mentoring.org/**

The National Mentoring Partnership works to help entire communities and states work together to sustain and expand mentoring opportunities for young people; schools, businesses, civic associations, faith communities and youth-serving organizations build or strengthen their mentoring programs; educators and work force preparation leaders integrate mentoring into programs; individuals learn about mentoring opportunities and become the mentors young people want and need.

Mirroring the National Mentoring Partnership's work, local partnerships are at the heart of the nationwide expansion of mentoring opportunities for young people. The local partnerships unite leaders around mentoring and, together, they recruit corporations, schools, faith communities and other organizations to develop mentoring programs; recruit and train adults how to become mentors; educate the public about mentoring; provide technical assistance and support to mentoring agencies; and secure resources.

> Mottahedeh Development Services
> 750 Hammond Dr.; Bldg. 12, Suite 300
> Atlanta, GA 30328; Phone: 404-843-1995
> Fax: 404-843-8895; Email: mdssed@msn.com
> URL: **http://www.mdssed.org/mds**

Mottahedeh Development Services was established by the National Spiritual Assembly of the Bahá'ís of the United States as a nonprofit agency to promote social and economic development to benefit individuals of any race, creed, or nationality. The agency name honors more than fifty years of dedicated service by Mildred and Rafi Mottahedeh, two pioneers in social and economic development. The Bahá'í Faith is a global religion with centers in more than two hundred countries and more than one hundred thousand communities all dedicated to the principles of the unity of religion, the oneness of mankind, the equality of the races, equality of men and women, and universal education. The Bahá'í International Community has consultative status as a nongovernmental organization with the U.N. Economic and Social Council and U.N. Children's Fund.

> Maryland Student Service Alliance
> Maryland State Department of Education
> 200 West Baltimore Street
> Baltimore, MD 21201; Phone: 410-767-0358
> URL: **http://www.mssa.sailorsite.net**

The courage to care, the strength to serve website from the Maryland Student Service Alliance provides support to public school students, teachers, administrators, and school districts to help them meet Maryland's service-learning high school graduation requirement.

> National Association for Public Interest Law (NAPIL)
> 2120 L Street, NW, Suite 450
> Washington, DC 20037; Phone: 202-466-3686
> Fax: 202-429-9766; Email: napil@napil.org
> URL: **http://www.napil.org/**

Thirteen years ago, law students from 15 different law schools joined together to form the National Association for Public Interest Law. They envisioned a unified organization that would promote public interest law on campuses and would increase paid public interest job opportunities. Today, NAPIL is doing just that. Over 150 law schools—more than 80% of all ABA-accredited schools—have NAPIL member groups that work on their campuses for public interest projects and raise over a million dollars a year for summer public-interest law scholarships. An annual NAPIL-sponsored career fair and conference connects thousands of law students with hundreds of public interest employers.

NAPIL's support for public interest employment opportunities continues beyond the law school campus, as NAPIL helps lawyers serve as advocates in often-forgotten communities. NAPIL administers the largest public interest legal fellowship program in the United States with 140 fellows currently in the field, and NAPIL coordinates federally funded national service programs that provide jobs for scores of other new lawyers. Through these programs, attorneys work for domestic violence victims, disabled children, Indian tribes, and other disadvantaged groups that otherwise could not afford legal help.

> National Association of PARTNERS IN EDUCATION
> 901 North Pitt Street, Suite 320
> Alexandria, VA 22314; Phone: 703-836-4880
> Fax: 703-836-6941
> URL: **http://www.napehq.org/**

For more than 30 years, National Association for Partners in Education has been an objective voice in developing school volunteer, intergenerational, community service, and business partnership programs throughout the United States. It is the only national membership organization devoted solely to the mission of providing leadership in the formation and growth of effective partnerships to ensure success for all students. In its effort to improve the academic and personal growth of all children, PARTNERS IN EDUCATION aims to increase the number, quality, and scope of effective partnerships; increase the availability of resources for the formation and support of effective partnerships; increase awareness about the importance of partnerships for promoting student success; and promote the importance of effective partnerships to policymakers.

National Association of Service and Conservation Corps (NASCC)
666 11th Street, N.W.
Suite 1000
Washington, DC 20001; Phone: 202-737-6272
Fax: 202-737-6277
URL: **http://www.nascc.org/**

The National Association of Service and Conservation Corps (NASCC) is the membership organization for youth corps programs. Since its inception in 1985 NASCC has served as an advocate, central reference point, and source of assistance for the growing number of state and local youth corps around the country. NASCC's primary mission is twofold: to strengthen the quality of existing youth corps programs and to promote the development of new ones.

Corporation for National Service//Learn & Serve America
1201 New York Avenue, NW
Washington, DC 20525; Phone: 202-606-5000
Email: webmaster@cns.gov
URL: **http://www.nationalservice.org/**

The Learn & Serve America National Service-Learning Clearinghouse is a comprehensive information system that focuses on all dimensions of service-learning, covering kindergarten through higher education school-based as well as community-based initiatives.

National Center for Education Statistics
555 New Jersey Avenue NW
Washington, DC 20208-5574; Phone: 202-219-1828
Fax: 202-219-1736
URL: **http://nces.ed.gov**

The purpose of the National Center for Education Statistics' website is to provide clear, complete information about NCES' mission and activities, and to serve the research and education community, as well as other interested communities. Part of the U.S. Department of Education, the National Center for Education Statistics (NCES) is the primary federal entity for collecting and analyzing data that are related to education in the United States and other nations. The National Center for Education Statistics fulfills a Congressional mandate to collect, collate, analyze, and report complete statistics on the condition of American education; conduct and publish reports; and review and report on education activities internationally.

URL: **http://nces.ed.gov/pubs99/1999043.pdf**

1999043 Service-Learning and Community Service in K–12 Public Schools service-learning, discussed here in terms of incorporating community service experiences into students' schoolwork, has long been viewed as a positive education reform option. Beginning in the 1970s, educators began paying more attention to this teaching option and the 1990s saw an array of initiatives to help promote the practice. To determine how extensive the practice is, NCES conducted the first national-level study of service-learning in America's K–12 public schools in the spring of 1999. Analysis of this study reveals a number of interesting results including the fact that roughly one-third of these schools have incorporated service-learning to some extent and that most of the schools that have service-learning provide teachers some sort of support to help them integrate service into their curriculum. September 28, 1999

URL: **http://nces.ed.gov/pubs99/1999007.pdf**

1999007 Indicator of the Month: Community service participation of students in grades 6–12. In 1996 about one half of students in grades 6–12 participated in community service, with 26 percent participating on a regular basis. Students were more likely to participate if their parents did so. April 19, 1999

URL: **http://nces.ed.gov/pubs99/1999131.pdf**

1999131 The Civic Development of 9th Through 12th Grade Students in the United States: 1996. Concern that the next generation of Americans may not be willing or able to engage in the democratic process has been growing. The report is designed to study this concern by focusing on five key factors associated with a desire and an ability to participate politically: levels of political knowledge; attention to politics; political participatory skills; degrees of political efficacy; and tolerance of diversity. These are collectively referred to as "measures of civic development" for the purposes of this report. All of the measures of civic development are found in the National Household Education Survey of 1996 Youth Civic Involvement component. The data collected in this survey allow civic development of 9th through 12th grade students to be studied in relation to their demographic characteristics, activities in and out of school, and family and school backgrounds. Of particular interest, because of its prominence in recent educational theory and national dialogues and legislation, is the relationship between students' participation in community service and their civic development. December 3, 1998

URL: **http://nces.ed.gov/pubs97/97331.html**
URL: **http://nces.ed.gov/pubs97/97331.pdf**

97331 Student Participation in Community Service Activity. This report examines data from the 1996 National Household Education Survey, Youth Civic Involvement component, in which students in grades 6 through 12 were asked about their participation in community service activities. Additionally, youth were asked about some of the ways that schools might encourage community service participation and integrate it with classroom learning. From these data, one can examine the relationship between community service participation and school practices, as reported by the students. The data also provide information about how participation in community service activities is related to student, family, community, and school characteristics. May 1, 1997

URL: **http://nces.ed.gov/pubs/95743.html**

95743 Community Service Performed by High School Seniors (Education Policy Issues: Statistical Perspectives). This brief provides information about the extent and nature of community service performed by students. A table presents percentages of high school seniors reporting any community service in the past two years by student characteristics and whether any of the service was required. November 6, 1995

National Civic League
1445 Market Street, # 300
Denver, CO 80202-1728; Phone: 303-571-4343
Fax: 303-571-4404
URL: **http://www.ncl.org/**

Founded in 1894 by Theodore Roosevelt, Louis Brandeis, and other turn of the century progressives, National Civic League is an advocacy organization vigorously promoting the principles of collaborative problem-solving and consensus-based decision making in local community building. NCL accomplishes its mission through technical assistance, training, publishing, research, and an awards program.

National Civic League//Alliance for National Renewal
Attn: ANR
1319 F Street NW, #204
Washington, DC 20004; Phone: 202-783-2961
Fax: 202-347-2161
URL: **http://www.ncl.org/anr/**

The Alliance for National Renewal (ANR) is a coalition of over 200 national and local organizations dedicated to the principles of community renewal. Their diverse group of Partners range from the Study Circles Resource Center in Pomfret, Connecticut—where a small staff has facilitated issue-based discussions in more than 70 communities—to the National 4-H Council and the 33 million member American Association of Retired Persons.

A catalyst for inspiring and helping citizens work together to improve their communities and thus, our nation, ANR offers assistance to communities that want to start community renewal alliances, access to a network of people who believe in taking back our nation, neighborhood by neighborhood, a collection of stories on successful community renewal efforts inspiration, ideas, tools and collaborative processes shared through conferences, publications, technical assistance, and the World Wide Web.

Study Circles Resource Center
PO Box 203
697 A Pomfret Street
Pomfret, CT 06258
URL: **http://www.ncl.org/anr/partners/scrc.htm**

The Study Circles Resource Center (SCRC) promotes small-group discussion programs, known as "study circles," on social and political issues. It assists communities in building coalitions to sponsor citizen-based discussion of issues such as race relations and violence. Publications are free or low-cost; consulting and networking services are provided at no charge.

National Council of Teachers of English
1111 W. Kenyon Road
Urbana, IL, 61801-1096; Phone: 1-800-369-6283
URL: **http://www.ncte.org/service/**

National Council of Teachers of English and Campus Compact make this site possible. It is focused on service-learning and writing instruction. The Service-Learning in Composition site includes program descriptions, teaching resources, community resources, research resources, etc. The site is customized to the need of college writing teachers, composition/rhetoric researchers, and community partners working on writing or literacy initiatives. The site is intended as a dynamic resource that will grow with the contributions of visitors. The pages are updated frequently in response to changing needs.

URL: **http://www.nicsl.coled.umn.edu/res/videos.htm**

National Service-Learning Clearinghouse has a direct link to a list of videos related to service-learning. The Clearinghouse does not distribute the videos, but have listed distributor contact information on the website.

National Wildlife Federation
8925 Leesburg Pike
Vienna, VA 22184; Phone: 703-790-4000
URL: **http://www.nwf.org**

The National Wildlife Federation focuses its work on specific core area environmental issues, endangered habitats, wetlands, sustainable communities, water quality, land stewardship, and international programs.

Eliza Earle, Project Coordinator,
ABCD Institute
2040 Sheridan Road, Evanston, IL 60208-4100; Phone: 847-491-8711
Fax: 847-467-4140
URL: **http://www.nwu.edu/IPR/abcd.html**

The Asset-Based Community Development Institute (ABCD) was established in 1995 by the Community Development Program at Northwestern's Institute for Policy Research. Its purpose is to proliferate the findings of John Kretzmann and John L. McKnight's two decades of research on capacity-building community development. To this end, a major focus of the ABCD Institute has been the production of resources and tools for community builders involved in the process of capacity-based initiatives, helping them identify, nurture, and mobilize neighborhood assets.

National Youth Leadership Council
1910 West County Road B
St. Paul, MN 55113; Phone: 651-631-3672
Fax: 651-631-2955; Email: nylcinfo@nylc.org
URL: **http://www.nylc.org**

The National Youth Leadership Council's mission is to engage young people in their communities and schools through innovation in learning, service, leadership, and public policy. As one of America's most prominent advocates of service-learning and youth service, the NYLC is at the forefront of efforts to reform education and guide enlightened youth-oriented public policy.

Karen Kollias, District Director
Martha Saunders, Assistant
Neighborhood Reinvestment Corp.
Latrobe Building
2 East Read Street, Fourth Floor
Baltimore, MD 21202-2470; Phone: 410-962-3181;
Fax: 410-962-7679; Email: msaunders@nw.org
URL: **http://www.nw.org/**

The Neighborhood Reinvestment Corporation, a national nonprofit, was created in 1978 by an act of Congress to revitalize America's older, distressed communities by establishing and supporting a national network of local nonprofit organizations. Neighborhood Reinvestment creates and strengthens resident-led partnerships of lenders, other businesspeople, and local government officials to revitalize and restore neighborhoods in decline.

URL: **http://www.opportunitynocs.org**

National Opportunity NOCS website, the Internet's leading resource for nonprofit jobs and employment opportunities. Job seekers can conduct free searches through our large database of available nonprofit jobs online, while nonprofit organizations can post help-wanted classified ads for job openings online. In addition to the jobs bank, National Opportunity NOCs also features a nonprofit library and career resource center. Opportunity NOCs has been a prominent source of nonprofit jobs since 1986. Published by The Management Center of San Francisco, California—with regional affiliates in Los Angeles, Dallas, Philadelphia, Atlanta, and Boston—National Opportunity NOCs is the Internet's leading human resource tool for careers in the arts, health, social services, education, and other public sector, social enterprise jobs.

The Office of University Partnerships
Clearinghouse/HUD USER
P.O. Box 6091
Rockville, MD 20849; Phone: 1-800-245-2691
Email: oup@oup.org
URL: **http://www.oup.org/**

The Housing and Community Development Act of 1992 required that, as part of the Community Outreach Partnership Centers (COPC) Program, HUD create a national clearinghouse to disseminate information on the program. In August of 1994, HUD, recognizing the importance of universities in local community building activities, created an Office of University Partnerships.

The Office is responsible for running five grant programs (the Community Outreach Partnership Centers Program, the Community Development Work Study Program, the Doctoral Dissertation Grant Program, the Hispanic-Serving Institutions Work Study Program, and the Hispanic-Serving Institutions Assisting Communities Program), including running competitions and fostering the creation of new partnerships. The University Partnerships Clearinghouse serves as a means to disseminate information about universities' many contributions to local community revitalization efforts.

Cornell PAR Network
c/o CaRDI
43 Warren Hall, Cornell University
Ithaca, NY 14853-7801; Phone: 607-255-1967
Fax: 607-255-9984
URL: **http://www.parnet.org/**

Based at Cornell University in the beautiful Finger Lakes region of central New York State, Participatory Action Research serves an international group of students, faculty, and other practitioners who share a commitment to promoting high standards of intellectual and social integrity in doing social research for social change.

Peace Corps
1111 20th Street NW
Washington, DC 20526; Phone: 1-800-424-8580
URL: **http://www.peacecorps.gov/home.html**

The history of the Peace Corps is the story of tens of thousands of people who have served as Volunteers since 1961. Their individual experiences—in the villages, towns, and cities of more than 130 countries—have composed a legacy of service that has become part of America's history.

After a day of campaigning for the presidency, John F. Kennedy arrived at the University of Michigan in Ann Arbor on October 14, 1960, at 2:00 a.m., to get some sleep, not to propose the establishment of an international volunteer organization. Members of the press had retired for the night, believing that nothing interesting would happen. But 10,000 students at the University were waiting to hear the presidential candidate speak, and it was there on the steps of the Michigan Union that a bold new experiment in public service was launched. The assembled students heard the future President issue a challenge: How many of them, he asked, would be willing to serve their country and the cause of peace by living and working in the developing world?

The reaction was both swift and enthusiastic, and over the last 37 years, more than 150,000 Americans have responded to this enduring challenge. And since then, the Peace Corps has demonstrated how the power of an idea can capture the imagination of an entire nation.

Pew Partnership
145-C Ednam Drive
Charlottesville, Virginia 22903; Phone: 804-971-2073
Fax: 804-971-7042; Email: mail@pew-partnership.org
URL: **http://www.pew-partnership.org/**

The Pew Partnership is a civic research organization whose mission is to document and disseminate cutting-edge community solutions. They collaborate with local and national partners to empower diverse leadership for action, catalyze broad-based community partnerships to solve problems, research successful community solutions and civic practices.

The Pew Partnership directs three national initiatives, one is Wanted: Solutions for America which is a call to the nation to identify, replicate, and celebrate what is working today to solve urgent community problems. Over the next three years, the Pew Partnership and a team of researchers will select 50 examples of successful solutions in cities, large and small, to share with the country. This "solutions" initiative will a) work with researchers to track the factors contributing to effective solutions; b) share cutting-edge strategies and proven tools, showcasing the best of research and practice, to national audiences; and c) increase the access communities and citizens have to information about tested solutions.

Another national initiative is the Pew Civic Entrepreneur Initiative (PCEI), which is spurring ten communities nationwide to broaden and deepen their leadership. The complexity of today's challenges demands that citizens from diverse backgrounds bring their expertise and experience to bear on the issues facing their communities. Each of the 10 PCEI cities selects 20 civic entrepreneurs annually to participate in a year of rigorous training in collaborative leadership.

The third initiative described here is the Civic Change Project, which launched collaborative, community problem-solving projects in 14 smaller cities tackling tough issues, such as at-risk youth, affordable housing, and jobs. From 1994–1996, each community was granted up to $400,000 to spearhead solutions to urgent problems in a long-term context. The Pew Partnership convened the participating communities twice yearly to share strategies and learn from nationally prominent practitioners. We also collaborated with the cities to provide ongoing targeted technical assistance. Finally, to help ensure the continuation of these projects, the Pew Partnership extended another $50,000 to each of eight cities in 1997.

The Massachusetts Public Interest Research Group
29 Temple Place
Boston, MA 02111; Phone: 617-292-4800
Fax: 617-292-8057; Email: masspirg@pirg.org
URL: **http://www.pirg.org/**

The Student Public Interest Research Groups, or PIRGs, were started 20 years ago by students wanting to study, learn about, and act on the pressing social problems of the day. PIRG Campus Chapters combine the energy and idealism of college students with the experience and expertise of a professional staff to promote the public interest.

Student PIRGs have registered hundreds of thousands of student voters, helped to pass the nation's most effective recycling laws, stopped Clean Water Act violators, strengthened the Clean Air Act, and promoted cutting-edge pollution prevention policies. PIRG student volunteers also organize community-service projects ranging from food and clothing drives to beach cleanups and waterway restorations.

PIRG campus chapters offer course credit internship opportunities that allow students to earn credit while working on structured projects with college faculty and PIRG professional staff. More than 100 colleges and universities across the country have PIRG Campus Chapters. Each chapter participates in projects at the local, state, and national levels. In addition to impacting important issues and learning civic skills, PIRG students gain valuable leadership experience. Each state PIRG is governed by a student Board of Directors, elected from each chapter. The student board is responsible for deciding the PIRG position on issues and the budget of the organization.

> The Points of Light Foundation
> 1400 I Street, NW Suite 800
> Washington, DC 20005; Phone: 202-729-8000
> Fax: 202-729-8100; Email: volnet@pointsoflight.org
> URL: **http://www.pointsoflight.com**

Founded in May 1990, the Points of Light Foundation is a nonpartisan, nonprofit organization devoted to promoting volunteerism. The Foundation is based in Washington, DC, and works in communities throughout the United States through a network of over 500 Volunteer Centers. Its Board of Directors includes prominent and politically diverse national leaders from business, education, and the nonprofit communities. Former President George Bush serves as the Honorary Chairman of the Board. The Foundation believes that, at the core of most social problems, lie disconnection and alienation, that is why the Foundation launched an initiative called Connect America. At the heart of this initiative is the idea that bringing people together through volunteer service is a powerful way of combating disconnection and alleviating social problems. A growing number of national membership-based organizations, corporations, cities and states are signing on to the Connect America movement by creating activities which unite people through volunteer service.

> URL: **http://www.pointsoflight.connectamerica/connectamerica.html**

Connect America is a national movement of a diverse group of national, state, and local organizations—nonprofit organizations, civic associations, businesses, fraternal organizations, communities of faith, government, news media, and volunteers—working in partnership to leverage knowledge, resources, and volunteers to address social and community problems. Connect America builds national public awareness about the power of connections through advertising, the media, and recognition efforts while demonstrating the outcomes of connections in addressing local social problems.

> URL: **http://www.pointsoflight.org/familymatters/default.htm**

Family Matters engages families in year-round community-oriented volunteer projects by linking families, neighborhoods, businesses, and nonprofits through FAMILY MATTERS' Clubs. Through research and extensive testing, FAMILY MATTERS has learned that family volunteering effectively strengthens the family, addresses critical social needs, improves employee morale within participating businesses, and creates a renewed community spirit. It makes a difference for individual families, large corporations, small neighborhoods, major metropolises, grassroots nonprofit agencies, and government institutions.

> President's Student Service Scholarships
> 1505 Riverview Road
> P.O. Box 68
> St. Peter, MN 56082; Phone: 888-275-5018
> Fax: 507-931-9168; Email: RDCSFA@aol.com
> URL: **http://www.student-service-awards.org**

Millions of students volunteer every day, improving communities and making America stronger. Launched this year, the President's Student Service Challenge is an opportunity for schools, colleges, and community organizations to recognize these young people for their outstanding community service and to encourage more young people to serve.

> National Commission on Civic Renewal
> Room 3111 Van Munching Hall
> University of Maryland
> College Park, MD 20742; Phone: 301-405-2790
> Fax: 301-314-9346
> URL: **http://www.puaf.umd.edu/civicrenewal/**

The National Commission on Civic Renewal, made possible by a grant from the Pew Charitable Trusts, will include individuals across the political spectrum and from many different walks of life, all of whom have demonstrated leadership in their fields and a commitment to the betterment of our country. The purpose of the Commission is to assess the condition of civic engagement in the United States today and to propose specific actions— to be undertaken by the public, private, and voluntary sectors as well as by individuals— that could improve this condition.

The Commission has been formed in response to a number of troubling trends in our civic life. During the past generation, the level of trust—in government, in large institutions, and in our fellow citizens—has fallen sharply. Basic civility has eroded, along with many kinds of civic participation. The content of our popular culture deeply troubles many of our citizens. Many Americans believe that the influence of religion in our society is lower than it once was and ought to be. The publication last year of Robert Putnam's now-famous essay, "Bowling Alone," has helped to crystallize fears that America's distinctive source of social strength—our network of voluntary associations—is weakening and has sparked an important scholarly debate.

> Public Allies Organization Wide Office
> 1015 18th Street, NW, Suite 200
> Washington, DC 0036; Phone: 202-822-1180
> Fax: 202-822-1199; Email: PANational@publicallies.org

Public Allies identifies a diversity of talented young adults and creates opportunities for them to practice leadership and strengthen their communities in a new alliance with people from neighborhoods, nonprofits, business, and government.

Pugwash USA
815 15th St., NW
Suite 814
Washington, DC 20005
Phone: 202-393-6555 or 1-800-WOW-A-PUG (students only, please)
Fax: 202-393-6550
URL: **http://www.igc.org/pugwash/**

Pugwash USA encourages young people to examine the ethical, social, and global implications of science and technology, and to make these concerns a guiding focus of their academic and professional endeavors.

Student Pugwash USA offers educational programs that are interdisciplinary, intergenerational, and international in scope, reflecting a belief that all citizens share a responsibility to ensure that science and technology are utilized for the benefit of humankind. Student Pugwash USA is guided by a respect for diverse perspectives and, as such, does not adopt advocacy positions on substantive issues.

Rock the Vote
10635 Santa Monica Boulevard
Box 22
Los Angeles CA 90025; Phone: 310-234-0665
Fax: 310-234-0666; Email: mail@rockthevote.org
URL: **http://www.rockthevote.org/**

Rock the Vote is dedicated to protecting freedom of expression and to helping young people realize and utilize their power to affect change in the civic and political lives of their communities.

Second Nature
44 Bromfield Street, Fifth Floor
Boston, MA 02108-4909; Phone: 617-292-7771
Fax: 617-292-0150; Email: info@secondnature.org
URL: **http://www.secondnature.org/**

Second Nature is a nonprofit organization working to help colleges and universities expand their efforts to make environmentally sustainable and just action a foundation of learning and practice. Education for Sustainability (EFS) is a lifelong learning process that leads to an informed and involved citizenry having the creative problem-solving skills, scientific and social literacy, and commitment to engage in reponsible individual and cooperative actions. Second Nature focuses on colleges and universities because they educate our future teachers, leaders, managers, policymakers, and other professionals.

SERVEnet
1101 15th Street, Suite 200
Washington, DC 20005; Phone: 202-296-2992
Email: feedback@ysa.org
URL: **http://servenet.org/**

SERVEnet is a program of Youth Service America. A leader in the field of youth service for more than 10 years, YSA continues its tradition of ground-breaking innovations in community service by supporting SERVEnet. SERVEnet is also the premier website for the service and volunteer field. SERVEnet is a free service that keeps you updated and involved in your community. SERVEnet brings thousands of volunteers and community organizations together online.

Service-Learning Research and Development Center
615 University Hall #1040
Berkeley, CA 94720-1040; Phone: 510-642-3199
Fax: 510-642-6105
URL: **http://www-gse.berkeley.edu/research/slc/servicelearning.html**

Service-Learning Research & Development Center, Graduate School of Education, University of California, Berkeley: the mission of the Service-Learning Center is to advance the service-learning field by furthering the understanding of service-learning through the development, implementation, facilitation, and evaluation of community service programs that are an integral part of the academic curriculum.

Service-Learning at the University of Colorado-Boulder
Campus Box 471
1201 17th Street,
IBS #5, Ste. 11
Boulder, CO 80309-0471; Phone: 303-492-7718
URL: **http://www.Colorado.EDU/servicelearning/**

Advice and guidelines to faculty, administration, students, and community members for beginning service-learning projects.

Special Olympics, Inc.
1325 G Street, NW/Suite 500
Washington, DC 20005; Phone: 202-628-3630
Fax: 202-824-0200
URL: **http://www.specialolympics.org/**

Special Olympics is a nonprofit program of sports training and competition for individuals with mental retardation. Founded in 1968 by Eunice Kennedy Shriver, Special Olympics provides year-round training and athletic competition for more than one million athletes in nearly 150 countries and all 50 states in the United States. Their mission is to provide year-round sports training and athletic competition in a variety of Olympic-type sports for individuals with mental retardation by giving them continuing opportunities to develop physical fitness, demonstrate courage, experience joy, and participate in a sharing of gifts, skills, and friendship with their families, other Special Olympics athletes and the community. Special Olympics believes that competition among those of equal abilities is the best way to test its athletes' skills, measure their progress, and inspire them to grow. Special Olympics believes that its program of sports training and competition helps people with mental retardation become physically fit and grow mentally, socially, and spiritually. Special Olympics believes that consistent training is required to develop sports skills.

Southern Poverty Law Center
400 Washington Avenue
Montgomery, Alabama 36104
URL: **http://www.splcenter.org/**

The Southern Poverty Law Center is a nonprofit organization that combats hate, intolerance, and discrimination through education and litigation. Its programs include Teaching Tolerance and Intelligence Project, which incorporates Klanwatch and the Militia Task Force. The Center also sponsors the Civil Rights Memorial, which celebrates the memory of 40 individuals who died during the Civil Rights Movement.

Kathy Sikes, Executive Director
Student Coalition for Action in Literacy Education (SCALE)
208 North Columbia Street
University of North Carolina at Chapel Hill
CB#3505
Chapel Hill, NC 27599-3505, Phone: 919-962-1542
Fax: 919-962-6020
URL: **http://www.unc.edu/depts/scale**

SCALE is a national organization that mobilizes college students to address the literacy needs of this country through partnerships with community agencies, service organizations, new readers, students, faculty, and administrators. SCALE's staff is composed of experienced literacy professionals, college students and recent graduates. College students, professors, new readers, literacy practitioners, and other social service activists make up SCALE's National Board of Advisors. SCALE is a member of the Center for Educational Leadership at the University of North Carolina at Chapel Hill.

SCALE offers training and technical assistance to college students working in the literacy field. SCALE works with both new and developing campus-based literacy groups, as well as existing organizations who wish to take their group to the next level. From ESL to child mentoring and adult literacy, SCALE provides the necessary support and resources to maintain a highly effective literacy program. SCALE runs a National Clearinghouse, the Area Campus Training Initiative, National Literacy Action Week, and a National Conference. Through SCALE's programs, students gain information, ideas, and skills to strengthen their work within local communities.

SCALE believes in increasing literacy for the transformation of individuals and society, as a vehicle for social justice. Increased literacy helps people to achieve their goals and empowers people to be more effective advocates both for themselves and their communities.

URL: **http://wwww.teachforamerica.org/main.htm**

Teach for America is the national corps of outstanding and diverse recent college graduates, of all academic majors, who commit two years to teach in under-resourced urban and rural public schools. Each year, over 1,000 corps members reach more than 100,000 students at thirteen locations across the country. Their alumni choose careers in many fields and continue as lifelong leaders in the pursuit of educational excellence for all children.

In 1999 1,300 top recent college graduates will teach in public schools in the most under-resourced areas of the nation as part of Teach For America. Corps members are proven leaders on their college campuses and in the communities where they serve. After their two-year teaching commitment, alumni continue applying their exceptional talent and experience inside and outside the classroom.

Teach for America select corps members for the qualities proven to make excellent teachers—an ability to thrive on overcoming challenges, a relentless drive to achieve results, a commitment to setting only the highest expectations for themselves and their students.

New corps members come together for an intensive five-week training program where they gain experience teaching while receiving guidance from veteran educators. They then travel to one of our thirteen urban or rural sites where school districts hire and pay them as regular beginning teachers (salaries range from $20,000 to $34,000). Local offices help orient corps members to their new schools and communities and foster professional and personal support networks.

After the two years, alumni continue working to expand educational opportunity through a variety of fields. Some remain in education, others continue their studies at leading graduate or professional schools, and still others work at top-notch organizations in the nonprofit, government, and corporate sectors. Teach For America helps keep alumni connected to each other, to Teach For America, and to their collective vision through local alumni chapters, on-line community newsletters, and national events.

TxServe
Texas Commission on Volunteerism & Community Service
P.O. Box 13385
Austin, TX 78711-3385
URL: **http://www.txserve.org/servlrn/servlrn.htm**

The Texas Center for Service-Learning at the University of Texas' Charles A. Dana Center provides technical assistance and facilitates training in service-learning for public school districts and campuses, institutions of higher education, nonprofit organizations (including private nonprofit schools), communities, businesses, and individuals. Our mission is to build sustainable communities through thoughtful service, reflective learning, and individual commitment.

MJCSL
University of Michigan
1024 Hill Street
Ann Arbor, MI 48109-3310
URL: **http://www.umich.edu/~ocsl/MJCSL/**

Michigan Journal of Community Service Learning is an important academic journal containing papers written by faculty and service-learning educators on research, theory, pedagogy, and issues pertinent to the service-learning community. Published articles include Sociology, Psychology, Engineering, Leadership, English and Peace Studies, among others.

Student Environmental Action Coalition
P.O. Box 31909
Philadelphia, PA 19104-0609; Phone: 215-222-4711
Fax: 215-222-2896; Email: seac@seac.org
URL: **http://www.seac.org/**

Student Environmental Action Coalition, SEAC, is a student- and youth-run national network of progressive organizations and individuals whose aim is to uproot environmental injustices through action and education. They define the environment to include the physical, economical, political, and cultural conditions in which we live. By challenging the power structure which threatens these environmental conditions, SEAC works to create progressive social change on both the local and global levels.

Through this united effort, thousands have translated the concern into action by sharing resources, building coalitions, and challenging the limited mainstream definition of environmental issues.

VFP International Workcamps
1034 Tiffany Road
Belmont, VT 05730-0202; Phone: 802-259-2759
Fax: 802-259-2922; Email: vfp@vfp.org
URL: **http://www.vfp.org**

Volunteers for Peace promotes International Voluntary Service as an effective means of intercultural education and community service. We provide programs where people from diverse backgrounds can work together to help overcome the need, violence and environmental decay facing our planet. Workcamps are truly the microcosm of a world where nations join together giving priority to improving life for humanity. They are a practical way to both prevent and resolve conflict.

Voluntary Service Overseas
317 Putney Bridge Road
London SW15 2PN, UK, Phone: (+44) 20 8780 7200
Fax: (+44) 20 8780 730
URL: **http://www.vso.org.uk/**

A "British-based volunteer-sending agency enabling people to share skills, build capabilities, and promote international understanding with poorer countries." They are two-year appointments.

URL: **http://www.volunteeramerica.net**

This website from Volunteer America, is dedicated to connecting individuals, families, and groups with volunteer opportunities on public lands all across America. On their web pages you will find hundreds of locations to volunteer. Some locations have volunteer opportunities posted, while others give an overview of a park, forest, historic site, or campground. You can submit an inquiry or volunteer application on-line, or print out their application and mail it to as many locations as you desire. Volunteer vacations or service trips accomplish work that would otherwise go undone. They allow ample time to enjoy the wilderness on your own. You couldn't ask for a better work environment. Some trips even include a short backpack after the work is done, or a break during the trip for day hikes, swimming, or just enjoying the vistas and views. Generally, no previous experience is required and your leaders will show you how it's done. The variety of tasks accommodates most levels of skill and stamina. They list hundreds of Volunteer Vacations or service opportunities sponsored by various organizations. Some organizations charge a small fee to participate, to offset the expenses of the trip, and you provide your own round-trip transportation. Sample trips: Humpback Whales Service Trip, Maui, Hawaii; Superstition Desert Wilderness Service Trip, Tonto National Forest, Arizona.

> Wilderness Volunteers
> P.O. Box 22292
> Flagstaff, AZ 86002; Phone: 520-556-0038
> Fax: 520-556-9664
> URL: **http://www.wildernessvolunteers.org/**

Organizes and promotes volunteer service to America's wild lands, primarily by co-ordinating trips to National Parks and Forests.

> Women In Community Service
> 1900 N. Beauregard St., Suite 103
> Alexandria, VA 22311; Phone: 703-671-0500 / 800-442-9427
> Fax: 703-671-4489; E-mail: WICSNatl@wics.org
> URL: **http://www.wics.org/**

Women In Community Service is an organization dedicated to reducing the number of young women living in poverty by promoting self-reliance and economic independence.

> Center for Youth as Resources
> National Headquarters
> 1700 K Street, NW, Suite 801
> Washington, DC 20006-3817; Phone: 202-261-4131
> Email: yar@ncpc.org
> URL: **http://www.yar.org/yar.htm**

The Center for Youth as Resources (CYAR) is a national nonprofit organization with offices in Washington, DC, and Indianapolis, IN, and serves as an umbrella organization for Youth as Resources (YAR) programs throughout the United States and abroad. Local YAR programs, governed by boards composed of youths and adults, provide grants for youth-initiated, youth-led community projects. The national CYAR board of directors is composed of youths and adults who work with staff to broadly promote the philosophy that youths are valuable community resources, and to advocate youth involvement in local, state, and national policy arenas. Through instructional materials, technical assistance, and hands-on training from experienced youths and adults, CYAR helps local YAR programs start, develop, and expand.

> YMCA of the USA, Association Advancement
> 101 North Wacker Drive
> Chicago, IL 60606; Phone: 312-977-0031
> URL: **http://www.ymca.net**

Young Men's Christian Association exists to build strong kids, strong families, and strong communities, and the national service system exists only to help empower YMCAs to achieve that vision. Their success on the national level lies in the superior achievement of member YMCAs. The effect of the national system is not measured by the number of conference reports, newsletters, or phone calls they handle. It is counted by the number of lives changed through what they do—the lives of the 57,000 volunteers who govern YMCAs nationwide and the lives of the hundreds of thousands of staff members and volunteers who carry out the work of their associations.

Lynn Riskedal, Ph.D.
Coordinator, Youth Curriculum Development/CYFERNet
University of Minnesota Extension Service
200 Oak St. SE Suite 270B
Minneapolis, MN 55455; Phone: 612-624-8113
Fax: 612-624-6905; Email: riske002@umn.edu;
URL: **www.4-H.org**

The 4-H Program was founded sometime between 1900 and 1910 to provide local educational clubs for rural youth from ages 9 to 19. It was designed to teach better home economics and agricultural techniques and to foster character development and good citizenship. The program, administered by the Cooperative Extension Service of the U.S. Department of Agriculture, state land-grant universities, and county governments, emphasizes projects the improve the four H's: head, heart, hands, and health.

Youth Service America
1101 15th Street, N.W.
Suite 200
Washington, DC 20005; Phone: 202-296-2992
URL: **http://www.ysa.org**

Youth Service America is a resource center and the premier alliance of 200+ organizations committed to increasing the quantity and quality of opportunities for young Americans to serve locally, nationally, or globally. YSA's mission is to strengthen the Effectiveness, Sustainability and Scale of the youth service movement. YSA envisions a powerful network of organizations committed to making service the common experience and expectation of all young Americans. A strong youth service movement will create healthy communities, and foster citizenship, knowledge, and the personal development of young people.

YSA has implemented the New Generation Training Program, which is a highly experiential and innovative national leadership development program. Since its inception, the two main objectives have been to provide skill-based training to meet the needs of young professionals and to create a network of young colleagues in the national and community service field. For more information visit: **http//ysa.org/ngtp/index.php3.**

Youth Service California
754 Sir Francis Drake, Suite 8
San Anselmo, CA 94960; Phone: 415-257-3500
Fax: 415-257-5838; Email: info@yscal.org
URL: **http://www.yscal.org**

Youth Service California supports, convenes and informs youth service programs and practitioners throughout California. Founded in 1990, Youth Service California (YSCal) is a nonprofit, statewide organization that promotes youth service and provides information and assistance to local programs across the State. Serving K–12 schools, institutions of higher education, conservation and service corps, Volunteer Centers, community-based organizations and committed individuals, YSCal acts as a convenor, networker, and promoter to build a statewide movement where young people are seen as powerful resources in meeting community needs. YSCal exists to support local programs and state agencies in making service part of every young person's experience in California.

URL: **http://www.upwithpeople.org/**

The purpose of Up With People is to develop the potential in people to bring the world together through friendship and understanding through an educational program that provides students with a unique global learning experience. This year-long program, known as Worldsmart, combines international travel, on-stage musical performance, and community service to accelerate education and career opportunities for students as they develop practical leadership skills for the future. After a year of gaining an incomparable breadth of knowledge, skills and wisdom, these students return home changed forever. They are now global citizens. They have become Worldsmart.

World Teach
c/o Center for International Development
Harvard University
79 JFK Street
Cambridge, MA 02138; Phone: 800-483-2240
Fax: 617-495-1599; Email: Info@worldteacher.org
URL: **http://www.worldteach.org/index.htm**

International social service program which places volunteers as teachers in developing countries that request educational assistance. Eight-week, six-month and full-year programs available.

URL: **http://www.yvca.org/adult.html**

Youth Volunteer Corps is looking for adults over the age of 18 to help organize and supervise their many volunteer service projects. If there is a YVC in your community, adult volunteers help supervise summer and school year service projects for middle school and high school age youth. Adult volunteers also help with transportation, recruitment of youth volunteers, and development of appropriate service projects.